M000317596

forty-four american boys

short histories *of* presidential childhoods

william walsh

Outpost19 | San Francisco
outpost19.com

Walsh, William
        Forty-four American Boys / William Walsh
        ISBN 9781944853259 (pbk)

Library of Congress Control Number: 2016918544

OUTPOST19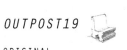

ORIGINAL
PROVOCATIVE
READING

Also by William Walsh

...reasons exist for being concerned with the early life of a president of the United States.

Even before achieving the presidency...a candidate for the office needs to offer the public a narrative of childhood that establishes a character, generates sympathy, and connects plausibly with his or her adult achievements. Although the style of presidential campaign biographies has changed over the years...publication of such biographies has been a constant feature of American elections almost from the beginning. Such biographies form the basis for later studies. Despite selective omission...they are generally accurate in outline...

— Hendrik Booraem
Child of the Revolution:
William Henry Harrison

- preface -

This book tells the story of the childhood of every American President to date through passages appropriated from more than 300 biographies, including children's books, pop history books, and scholarly works.

Each chapter is told without naming the boy who would later become President. In this way, the narratives are more broadly about boyhood in America. Also, there's a pronoun constraint at play throughout the book: Each sentence is controlled by he, his, or him.

Readers will note that Chapter 24 is presented as ditto. That's because the boy who grew up to be America's 24th President was also its 22nd. Since he served two nonconsecutive terms, he is considered to be the 22nd and 24th President.

- one -

He was a product of his father's second marriage.

The little boy born February 22, 1732, in the tidewater area of Virginia, had a knack for making it against the odds.

He had been born a British subject, as had everyone born in the thirteen American colonies. He had five brothers and a sister, so he had a very large family growing up!

He was a fourth-generation Virginian. His sparsely docu-mented early years have subsequently been littered with legends and lore, all designed to align his childhood with either the dramatic achievements of his later career or the mythological imperatives of America's preeminent national hero.

What can be seen in him with great clarity is that his overweening ambition was visible from an early age. His childhood was a roving and unsettled one.

He learned etiquette as well, some of it from *The Rules of Civility, and Decent Behavior in Company and Conversation*, a century-old collection of 110 maxims of gentlemanly behavior that he found somewhere and copied in his own hand. He took pride in his penmanship.

His mother drilled habits of thrift and industry into all of her children, including rising early with the sun, a strict farmer's habit that he retained for the rest of his life.

Death first encroached on his life when, right before his third birthday, his older half-sister Jane died.

In 1735, when he was three, his father relocated the family sixty miles upstream to a 2,500-acre tract at Little Hunting Creek on the Potomac, an unspoiled area of pristine forests.

There was nothing cosseted about his provincial boyhood, and he had little exposure to any pampered society that might have softened the rigors of his rural upbringing.

The meadow was his play-ground, and the scene of his early athletic sports.

Six years old, he climbed his favorite oak tree and scanned the horizon. He could see the swirling waters of Little Hunting Creek emptying into the mile-wide Potomac River. Four ships, majestic with their sails billowing in the stiff breeze, maneuvered their way along the river. He knew the ships had come from England, across the Atlantic Ocean, through Chesapeake Bay, and on up the Potomac. And now, as they sailed past Epsewasson, he could make out sailors standing on their aft decks.

He hiked seven miles to school and back until he was twelve years old. He loved the outdoors, particularly fishing and foxhunting. In adolescence he underwent a metamorphosis from a callow youth into a more polished young man.

He had once had his heart set on being an officer in the British army.

He had intended to go to the same school his father and older half-brothers had gone to—Appleby, in England. However, there wasn't enough money left for him to follow in their footsteps after his father died.

But before he would be ready for school anywhere, he needed to learn to read, write, and do math. So when he was seven years old, his parents decided he was ready to start learning. His mother taught him the basics of reading and writing and how to add and subtract numbers. After this, he began attending a small school in Fredericks-burg, where he enjoyed learning how to draw maps most of all.

He read to learn about the world, as well as to implant in his mind a vision of the kind of person he wanted to become. He didn't skim books to prepare for an exam. He read fewer books than his brothers had read, but he read them more deeply. For him, reading was a privilege, a key he used to understand the world and expand his mind and horizons.

He loved to stand at his bedroom window and gaze across the river to Fredericksburg. Watching the barges being loaded and unloaded, he could hardly wait until the time when he would be climbing aboard a ship and setting sail for England to attend school.

Down by the ferry dock, he watched as goods such as wood, rice, indigo dyes, tobacco, and animal furs were loaded on to barges to be taken downriver to be loaded onto ships bound for England. The barges would return upriver, he knew, laden with clothing, glass, clocks, books, kettles, and carpenters' tools from England.

His father had planted an orchard of fine fruit trees: there were apple trees, peach trees, pear trees, plum trees, and cherry trees. One very special cherry tree came to his father from across the ocean. His father planted it on the edge of orchard, and he told everyone on the farm to watch it carefully to see that it was not broken or hurt in any way. He watched his father's cherry tree grow and blossom in the spring. His father was pleased that the family would soon have cherries from the little tree. Just about this time, his father gave him a shiny new hatchet. He took it and went about chopping sticks, hacking into the rails of fences, and cutting whatever else he passed. At last he came to the edge of the orchard, and thinking only of how well his hatchet could cut, he chopped into the little cherry tree. The bark was soft, and it cut so easily that he chopped the tree right down and went on with his play. That evening, when his father came from inspecting the farm, he sent his horse to stable and walked down to the orchard to look at the cherry tree. His father stood in amazement when he saw how it was cut, and he wondered, Who would have dared do such a thing? When no one on the farm

3

could say what had happened to the cherry tree, his father asked him, in an angry voice, Do you know who killed my cherry tree? He was staggered under for a moment by his father's question, but he recovered quickly and answered, I cannot tell a lie, father; I did it with my hatchet.

Although he was a superb physical specimen, with a magnificent physique, his family's medical history was blighted by truncated lives.

He was eleven when his father died. He inherited parcels of land and ten slaves.

With painstaking effort, he learned to write in a round hand that lacked elegance but had great clarity. It took him time to compose clean, declarative sentences—his teenage prose was often turgid and ungrammatical—but by dint of hard work, his powers grew steadily until he became a writer of considerable force, able to register his wishes with precision.

His manuscript schoolbooks still exist, and are models of neatness and accuracy. One of them, it is true, a ciphering book, preserved in the library of Mount Vernon, has some of his schoolboy attempts at calligraphy; nondescript birds, executed with a flourish of the pen, or profiles of faces, probably intended for those of his schoolmates; the rest are all grave and business-like.

He had seen his brother fitted out for the wars. All his amusements took a military turn. He made soldiers of his schoolmates; they had their mimic parades, reviews, and sham fights.

He inherited from his mother a high temper and a spirit of command, but her early precepts and example taught him to restrain and govern that temper, and to square his conduct on the exact principles of equity and justice.

It was his nature to make the most of experience and observation and learn from his mistakes.

Before he was thirteen years of age he had copied into a volume forms for all kinds of mercantile and legal papers; bills of exchange, notes of hand, deeds, bonds, and the like. His early self-tuition gave him throughout life a lawyer's skill in drafting documents and a merchant's exactness in keeping accounts.

He never had a formal education. What he learned was practical—arithmetic, or ciphering, as it was called, geography, surveying, and etiquette. He received the modern equivalent of a grade-school education, but was never exposed to the classical curriculum or encouraged to attend William and Mary, a deficiency that haunted him throughout his subsequent career among American statesman with more robust educational credentials.

He was a superb rider. His fellow Virginian, Thomas Jefferson said he was "the best horseman of his age and the most graceful figure that could be seen on horseback."

He got his first job—assisting a surveyor who was laying out the town of Alexandria—when he was sixteen. He kept notes, watched the surveyor as he worked, hunted wild turkeys, lived in a tent, cooked over an open fire. He acquired a love for the west and decided to pursue a career as a surveyor. In July 1749, he was named official surveyor of the newly formed Culpepper County.

By his late teens, he stood six feet two inches, taller than most men at that time. He had light blue eyes, auburn hair, and, contemporaries said, the largest hands and feet they had ever seen.

In September 1751, he travelled to Barbados where he attended the theater for the first time, exulted in the "beautiful prospects" of the island, and then became ill with smallpox. He did not fully recover until mid-December. It left him with a few pockmarks on his face and an immunity that was to prove a blessing.

- two -

The first fifteen years of his life went off like a fairy tale.

He was born in Braintree, Massachusetts in October of 1735. His family had lived in the quiet village for a hundred years. His father was his idol.

He lived with his family on a peaceful farm. He hated to leave home.

He had two younger brothers, and although they all looked alike, with curly blond hair and bright blue eyes, the two younger boys were destined for a life totally different from his.

Taught to read at home, he went first and happily to a dame school—lessons for a handful of children in the kitchen of a neighbor, with heavy reliance on *The New England Primer*.

A good-looking, active boy, if small for his age, he was unusually sensitive to criticism but also quickly responsive to praise, as well as being extremely bright, which his father saw early, and decided he must go to Harvard to become a minister.

As a boy, he loved to roam the woods and fields. He loved to walk along sandy beaches. He liked to fly kites. He loved making toy boats and sailing them in Fresh Brook. More than anything, he loved America.

He and his friends wrestled and shot marbles, and when the long, bitter winters plummeted onto New England, he searched out a frozen pond where he could skate, oblivious, as only children can be, to the numbing winds and torturous temperatures.

He loved hunting in the marsh, shooting well. Bringing down

game for the table. He patrolled the region about Braintree until he was familiar with every eddy and hill. He often trekked through waist-high brush, hoping to scare out a rabbit, or he plunged deep into the woods, hiding in an alcove near an abundance of oaks, waiting silently for a squirrel to appear, straining to hear a rasping bark or the muted scratching of a forager.

He seemed addicted to the outdoors.

He was under a bundle of reeds next to a little marsh island and flock of ducks. They were painted wooden ducks that he had carved out of cedar and pine. He hoped that real ducks would see them and think this marsh was a good place for a rest and some food. He struggled to be quiet and patient, but he was worse than almost anybody in Massachusetts at silence and patience.

He was a truant repeatedly, often sneaking away in midmorning to hunt or fish. When he told his father it was his teacher he disliked, not the books, and that he wished to go to another school, his father immediately took his side and wasted no time with further talk, enrolling him the next day in a private school down the road.

He had Ponkapoag Indian friends. In the summer when their tribe fished and dug clams at the seashore, he'd seen old men return the clamshells and fish bones to the water after the tribe had eaten.

Beyond the dunes and tidal flats to the north, was the great city of Boston, where as many as ten thousand people lived. Eastward across the marsh, were Massachusetts Bay and the Atlantic Ocean. He had heard some folks say that a squirrel could start in the maple and spruce woods of the Blue Hills and travel from tree to tree all the way to the fabled Mississippi River without ever touching the ground.

He imagined his ancestors sailing across the Atlantic Ocean to

Plymouth, twenty-five miles to the south of Braintree. He was proud of his ancestors.

He was thirteen years old, and by now most of his friends in Braintree had left school and were helping their fathers on their family farms.
He cared not for books or study, and saw no sense in talk of college. He wished only to be a farmer, he informed his father.

In a little more than a year, at age fifteen, he was pronounced "fitted for college," which meant Harvard, it being the only choice. His father sold ten acres of land to help pay for college.

He was an admirable specimen of the New England Puritan of his generation, not excessively strait-laced in matters of doctrine, but religious by habit and by instinct, rigid in every point of morals, conscientious, upright, pure-minded, industrious.

He worked hard and did well at Harvard, and was attracted particularly to mathematics and science. He enjoyed his classmates and made several close friends. He was short and stout. He was argumentative and blunt. He sometimes got along with almost no one.

He liked to talk and talk. He joined a debating club so that he could talk some more. To his surprise, he also discovered a love of study and books such as he had never imagined. Having discovered books at Harvard, he was seldom ever to be without one for the rest of his days.

He was reputed to be a very good scholar, but cannot be accurately compared to his comrades, since rank was not then given for scholarship.

When he graduated in 1755, he took a teaching job. He taught school by day and studied law at night.

At age twenty he began to realize that he harbored an enduring commitment to being highly reputed, saying that he craved "Honour or Reputation" and "more deference from fellows." At age twenty-one he contemplated expectations of becoming "a great Man." After much reflection, he decided to become a lawyer to further those ends, writing his father that he found among lawyers "noble and gallant achievements" but among the clergy, the "pretended sanctity of some absolute dunces."

- three -

By birth he was an aristocrat, by nature he was a democrat.

Born in April of 1743, he was the direct descendant of Welsh kings. He was the third of ten children. He was trained for greatness from the very beginning.

His father was a surveyor and cartographer whose immigrant parents were said to have come from the Snowdonia district of northern Wales.

His mother was the daughter of a ship's captain.

According to family tradition, his earliest memory was of a trusted slave carrying him, at the age of two, on a pillow when his family moved from his birthplace, the Shadwell plantation, to the Tuckahoe plantation, along the James River above Richmond.

He loved books. He read all of this father's books before the age of five. He was interested in everything—like science and art and music and farming and language and law and government. He inherited from his father a love of mathematics and of literature. He loved flowers growing and fish in the pond. Another way of saying this is he loved flora and fauna.

He didn't skip school. He skipped recess—to study Greek grammar.

He was an irrestrainable student, sometimes studying twelve and fourteen hours out of the twenty-four. His inquisitiveness was proverbial in his neighborhood. Early acquaintances remembered his insistence on seeing and understanding everything around him.

His hair was sandy of color, his cheeks ruddy, his eyes of a light hazel, his features angular, but glowing with intelligence. He was tall and lean. He was soft-spoken and polite. He got along with just about everyone.

He loved dancing, playing the violin. He sometimes practiced his violin up to three hours a day.

He was shy and dreaded speaking in front of crowds. Talking too loudly made his voice hoarse. He hated arguments. If he had an idea, he quietly wrote it down.

His father was the owner of thirty slaves and of a wheat and tobacco farm of nearly two thousand acres. He was certainly becoming aware of the enforced differences between blacks and whites without being formally taught. One of the inequities of the system was driven home when his father permitted him to go to school on the plantation while his black playmates could not.

He had two tutors, one whom he detested, the other he honored. He had religion drummed into him by his tutors. He was brought up as an Episcopalian; but as a young man he ceased to believe in Christianity as a religion.

Prodded into a horse race with a classmate, he realized that his slow pony stood little chance against his classmate's swift mare. So he cleverly suggested that the race be postponed until February 30. All the boys looked forward to the race with excitement, and not until the last day of the month did it dawn on them that he had duped them all.

By the age of fourteen, he could read Greek, Latin, and French literature in the original. He devoured books by Homer, Plato, Livy, and Cicero, read in Latin.

He read about shrews and shows and bees and cheese and how to say please in French, Spanish, Latin, Greek, Italian, German and English of course.

He liked to hike in the woods, but not to hunt. He was not graceful on his feet, but he learned to ride boldly and wonderfully.

One day, his father turned him loose in the woods with a gun to learn self-reliance, insisting that he bring home a wild turkey for dinner. Unable to find any of the elusive birds on the wing he found a penned-up turkey, tied it to a tree with his garter, shot it, and hauled it home without comment.

In the spring of 1760, he set out on horseback for Williamsburg, the capital of Virginia, where he proposed to enter the college of William and Mary. He was seventeen when he entered college and was one of "gawkiest" students. He was tall, growing fast, raw-boned, with prominent chin and cheekbones, big hands and feet, sandy-haired and freckled.

He graduated a mere two years later.

He was like a fine horse, he had no surplus flesh. He had an iron constitution, and was very strong.

He learned to dance minuets, reels, and country dances like any other Virginia gentleman, if somewhat more awkwardly. His favorite amusement, his passion, was to play the violin, not only by ear but by sight reading.

He loved conversation, but he couldn't make a speech; mumbling, he became tongue-tied when he made extemporaneous remarks.

When he encountered a neighbor or stranger doing something he did not understand, he asked questions and observed the proceedings until his curiosity was fully gratified, and then usually made notes of his observations in a memorandum book.

His father taught him how to carefully measure and survey land, a practical skill for any man, but especially for a lad who would one day possess his own lands.

He was always proud of his father. His father was considered the strongest man physically in the county, and the son grew to be like him in that respect, but the elder died while the younger was a boy. He missed his father terribly, and he transferred his grief into blaming his mother.

His father's death staggered him. He felt "the whole care and direction of myself was thrown on myself entirely." He buried himself in a refuge of books and music, seeking comfort.

If he heard a piece played on the harpsichord, he could transpose the notes for violin. On visits home from school, he loved to accompany his favorite sibling, Jane, while she sang.

He studied law and became a lawyer in Virginia in 1767.

When he was twenty-one, he began building his own house. He had some knowledge of architecture, so he designed his home himself. He called it Monticello. Which means 'little mountain' in Italian. He began working on it in 1768, but he did not finish it for a long time. He kept changing, changing, changing the house all the time. He gave the house seventy-six windows to let the light and air in.

- four -

By chance, he was an American Prince.

He was born in Orange County, in the British Colony of Virginia, on the 5th of March, 1750; or according to the Gregorian calendar, adopted the year after that of his birth, on the 16th of March, 1751, of a distinguished and opulent family.

He was named after his father, and his parents prepared for his homecoming by having a woodworker make a cradle.

He knew nothing of his ancestors before their arrival in America.

He grew up as the oldest of twelve children. He grew up in a family as large as an oyster bed: good training for a future lawmaker.

The account thus obtained is necessarily conjectural in some of its details, so something of an otherwise hidden boyhood assumes sketchy form.

We do not need to imagine him struggling against obscurantism or poverty to gain an education. His parent had the means and inclination to provide their children with a sound though simple education and their eldest son took full advantage of what was available.

At nine he was reading, and although he had always asked questions of his own (Where do the red birds fly in winter?), he was discovering in his father's library questions he would never have thought if asking.

He was not physically imposing.

He was naturally reserved. He did not leap forward to meet

strangers or try to dominate in conversation.

He was small for his age and had a voice as wispy as the wind.

If he tried to shout, the shout shriveled up in his throat, but of course he was still young. His voice might grow as he did. Or he might never need a big voice.

He knew that his Grandfather's slaves had built their house.

He grew up to love the outdoors and probably spent much of his boyhood riding and playing in the fields and forests with his brothers and the slave children on the plantation, but he was also bookish.

The future president's reading included books from his father's modest library and articles from Joseph Addison's *The Spectator*, a popular magazine known for its elegant essays. From *The Spectator*, a London periodical that he favored in his early years, he had learned that modesty becomes a man.

As the eldest, he had to set an example, tend his siblings, uphold his father's authority before relatives and slaves, responsibilities he assumed with entire loyalty.

Here he was, eleven years old and there was not another book in the house to read. He learned French so he could read books that were written in French and he learned Latin and Greek so he could find out what men thought hundreds of years ago.

The number of slaves the family owned grew rapidly; by 1782 there were at least 118.

He would read about Prince Eugene of Savoy, who, said *The Spectator*, exemplified "the highest instance of a noble mind," bearing "great qualities" without displaying "any consciousness that he is superior to the rest of the world."

He studied geometry and algebra and the history of other

nations, and to show just how much bigger his notion of the world had become, he drew a picture of the universe in his copybook.

For years his health suffered from over-application to books, or was it from the climate, or from poor eyesight in an age of incorrect lenses in spectacles?

He also suffered from psychosomatic, or stress-induced, seizures, similar to epileptic fits, that plagued him on and off throughout his youth.

As he grew older, he wrote essays that digested what he had learned.

He learned some Hebrew, a prerequisite for the ministry, though he seems to have had no intention of preaching.

He didn't look old enough to be going to college, although actually he was older than most. His face had that young, unset, waiting look. And he was little. At five-feet six, he was not excessively short, but because he was thin with a slight build and narrow shoulders, people were forever remarking on his littleness. His voice was little too. Moreover, he was shy.

At Princeton he was known for writing poetic satires. His poems were often mildly vulgar.

He turned out essays as clear as a Blue Ridge Mountain stream. It was the speaking part that troubled him. He could not bring himself to speak up in class. It was that little wispy voice of his, he told his teacher.

As the scion of a prominent planter family, he—unlike most Virginia boys—received an enviable education.

In the middle of a parched summer, he, eighteen years old, left the Virginia upcountry for Princeton, accompanied by his tutor and an enslaved man named Sawney, who was also eighteen.

He had performed well enough in Latin and Greek on his entrance exams to be able to skip his freshman year. Working his way through sophomore studies, he had looked ahead to his junior and senior years and decided he could do both at once, a course that his father might have encouraged. In the end, he might have decided that not only was he smart enough to shorten his time at Princeton but doing so was a way to save his father money.

He dressed plainly. Eventually, he would only wear black. His public speaking was as unadorned as his dress.

Although he would later win acclaim for his learnedness, he was never a cold, calculating scholar. Rather, he always demonstrated an active sense of humor. Proof of this from his college days is provided by some poetry he contributed to an intramural dispute.

At Princeton, he imbibed strong republican sentiments as well as a skeptical attitude toward officeholders.

- five -

He was born on April 28, 1758
near the head of Monroe's Creek,
in the Northern Neck of Virginia.

There was great joy in the house when he was born.

His father owned about five hundred acres of land in Westmorland County, Virginia. His family's property was not like the grand plantations owned by some of their neighbors.

His mother was a very amiable and respectable woman, possessing the best domestic qualities of a good wife, and a good parent.

He was of French and Scottish descent.

As a baby, he did not cry often. In fact, he was a rather quiet child. From the first, he seemed to think things through before doing anything. He was happy to play quietly, by himself or with his sister.

When he was big enough to walk, he roamed freely with his sister over the farm and through the surrounding woods.

When he was four, he fed farmyard animals; at six, he raked and hoed the kitchen garden; he picked vegetables and fruit at seven, milked cows at eight—and so on into his early teens, when he grew strong enough to handle the plow and plow horse.

From childhood, he and his sister were alike in many ways, and they remained close friends throughout their lives.

His mother and father taught him to read, write, and calculate, using the Scriptures and a variety of literature and periodicals.

His formal education began at eleven, when he was enrolled as a day student at Campbelltown Academy, a school operated by the Rev. Archibald Campbell, rector of Washington Parish.

He trekked five miles through icy woods to school each day, rising before dawn, carrying books under one arm and a musket slung over his shoulder.

He was accompanied on his long, woods-lined walks to Parson Campbell's school by his neighbor and friend John Marshall, the future chief justice of the United States. With his schoolbooks in mathematics and Latin, he also carried a frontier rifle.

His childhood was carefree and pleasant. His parents were loving and his world was secure. His family grew their own vegetables, raised chickens, geese, and pigs, and kept cows for milk, butter, and cheese.

In addition to farming, his father earned money as a joiner, or house builder.

He sailed, he fished, he rode, he followed the hounds and bird dogs. Probably he was out and about with the black boys much of the time.

He cherished no sentimental attachment for the scenes of his youth in the humid Tidewater, where, like most plantation-bred young men, he was allowed great freedom, acquiring a lasting enthusiasm for such active pursuits as riding and hunting.

He was but fourteen when his mother died.

He developed a steady interest in the round of agricultural activities upon which the well-being of his family and of the colony had so long depended.

Like other farm boys, he attended school only about twelve

weeks a year, between the last fall harvest and the first spring planting when there as little work in the fields of pastures.

He was so thoroughly drilled in Latin and mathematics that when he entered William and Mary in 1774 he was at once admitted into the upper or college division. As a student, he participated in minor incidents between the Virginians and the British.

Upon the death of his father in 1774, he inherited his small plantation and slaves.

A year later, he left college and joined the American cause in the Revolution by enlisting in the Third Virginia Infantry. He was seventeen years of age at the first formation of the American army and entered it as a cadet.

He received a commission as a lieutenant. After training in Virginia, the Third Infantry moved to New York and there joined the main American force near Manhattan.

He soon fell under the eye of General George Washington.

On the evening of Christmas day, 1776, he was with General George Washington when he commanded his army to cross the semi-frozen Delaware River for a surprise attack on Trenton at dawn the next day. He was in the front of this movement, leading the Third Virginia Infantry. As he led his troops, he was shot through the shoulder. He probably would have bled to death had he not received immediate medical care. He spent a month recuperating.

He was a war hero, a fighting soldier, and he played brave parts at Brandywine, Germantown, and Monmouth. He participated in the battles of Harlem Heights and White Plains, and in the retreat through New Jersey to Pennsylvania. He was at the encampment at Valley Forge. Although he remained in the army and was promoted to the rank of captain, he played a minor role for the rest of the war.

Most likely the romance, the fascination of history, got into his blood; and along with it that Lafayette-like love of liberty which ever after characterized him.

At any rate, it is clear that he breathed in Americanism with his first conscious breath. He sprang from stock that was native to American soil at least a hundred years before the War of the Revolution. Whatever was foreign in him had been bred out; he was truly a son of the western world, altogether rid of alien preconceptions, and quite ready to take on the plantation democracy of the seventeen-seventies and the new doctrines of his age.

In 1780, at the advice of Governor Thomas Jefferson, he reentered William and Mary where he studied law.

- six -

He was born during the early events of the American Revolution, on July 11, 1767.

His mother and father were distant cousins.

When he was three years old he fractured his finger. His doctor, an exemplary physician and close family friend, saved it from amputation.

When he was seven, he wrote a letter to his father, who was in Philadelphia as a representative of Massachusetts to the Continental Congress. The letter said, "I have been trying ever since you went away to learn to write you a letter. I shall make poor work of it, but…Mamma says…my duty to you may be expressed in poor writing as well as good. I hope I grow a better boy and that you will have no occasion to be ashamed of me when you return."

In a letter from the Continental Congress, his father wrote: "I wish to turn your thoughts early to such studies as will afford you the most solid instruction and improvement for the part which might be allotted you to act on the stage of life (since) the future circumstances of your country, may require other wars as well as councils and negotiations, similar to those which are now in agitation."

He learned nothing that he could not respect about his ancestors.

Before the war, his days had been partly a pastoral idyll.

He learned a lot from his father who became the second president of the United States.

In the early morning of June 17, 1775, he and his mother climbed a hill behind their farm in Braintree. The roar of cannon fire had awakened him. From the hilltop, he and his mother could see a battle raging around Bunker Hill and Breed's Hill on a finger of land on the far side of Boston, and the British burning of Charlestown.

His mother was known for melting pewter tableware to make bullets from the Continental Army during the war.

He liked the sound of his mother's goose quill scratching black ink across white paper.

His big sister was named after their mother, but she looked like their stocky father. Being the oldest, she was bossy sometimes, but he mostly liked her.

He didn't have a very normal childhood. When he started his education it wasn't at the local school. Assistants from his father's law office became his teachers. His progress in French even made his father jealous.

Most of his teachers agreed that he was a genius.

After a fearful six-week voyage in early 1778, his European education began. While his father negotiated with French officials, he attended boarding school. He studied not only Latin and French, but also dancing, fencing, music, and drawing.

His parents justified the trip to France as an opportunity to for him to learn more. In Braintree he had had home schooling, effective but limited. Now the urbanity of Paris provided new vistas, an actual school, and city attractions.

Within days of landing in Paris in early April 1778, he was immersed in his own activities. His eyes were on the attraction of the city, his new friends, and the school he began attending.

When he was fourteen, he travelled to Europe again to serve as a translator and secretary for an American diplomat. The mission brought him through Germany, Russia, Sweden, and Denmark.

During the voyage, his ship was chased by British warships.

He remained in Europe through the end of the war. In 1784 his father was named United States minister to Great Britain. He was reunited with his family in London. When he appeared at their hotel, he was no longer the boy they remembered, but a seventeen-year-old man.

His father called him "the greatest traveler of his age, and...I think as promising and manly a youth as is in the world."

He was bothered by what he saw in Russia. It seemed like everyone he saw there was either very, very rich or very, very poor.

During his extended stay on the continent, he adopted many European ways, including a large wardrobe with sixty-five pairs of stockings and numerous suits. He was not a flashy dresser, however—the suits were nearly all blue or black.

He learned to play the flute and refined his talents in writing and public speaking.

In letters home, he listed for his mother the sights that every visitor needed to see, the "scenes of Magnificence from the Palace and Gardens of Versailles" to "the Church of Notre Dame," many of which he visited in his father's company.

He roamed Paris by himself or with friends. At Versailles, he had the distinction of being his father's son, an introduction that accompanied him in most of his activities and that gave his father the pleasure of seeing his eleven-year old performing with a dignity and courtesy that evoked expression of praise from their French hosts.

To him, Parisian theater was fascinating, different from any experience available in Boston, where performing plays was forbidden.

He wrote to an American cousin, "I have been such a wandering being these seven years, that I have never performed any regular course of studies, and am deficient in many subjects. I wish very much to have a degree at Harvard." His father had also studied at Harvard.

In 1785 he returned to the United States by himself, seeking a different kind of education in the land of his birth.

Harvard admitted him as a junior. He loved his studies but had little respect for his instructors.

After Harvard, he became a lawyer. He became a lawyer to please his father. His heart was never really in it, though.

He began writing clever newspaper articles that supported the way the nation's first president, George Washington, was doing his job. President Washington appreciated his reports and offered him a job as a United States diplomat in the Netherlands. His father, who was vice president at the time, was very proud of him.

- seven -

He was born on March 15, 1767 in the
Waxhaw region, an area along the border
between North Carolina and South Carolina.

His father died in an accident three weeks before his birth.

His mother was a woman of strong character, who cherished for
her last-born the desire that he should become a Presbyterian
clergyman.

His ancestors lived in the Irish county of Antrim, in or near the
town of Carrickfergus.

Little is authentically known of his early years. The question is of
less importance than the fact, of which there is no question, that
he was born to the humblest circumstances in a new settlement
of a new country, and that his childhood and boyhood were
passed among people of little culture, whose lives were hard
and bare.

As he learned to talk and otherwise express himself, he showed
every sign of being the brightest of his mother's three children
and the most likely to master the literary arts required of a man
of the cloth.

He was a wild child, with an almost unmanageable will and a
defiant temper. He grew up an outsider, living on the margins
and at the mercy of others.

He struggled against poverty as a child, against authority as a
youth. His struggles defined him.

He was ready for a frolic or a fight at any hour of the day or night; he excelled in such sports as required swiftness and nerve.

He was mischievous, willful, daring, reckless. He was fond of practical jokes; he was not overfond of study.

Of education the boy received only such as was put unavoidably in his way. It is said that his mother taught him to read before he was five years old; and he attended several terms in the little low-roofed log schoolhouse in the Waxhaw settlement. But his formal instruction never took him beyond the fundamentals of reading, writing, geography, grammar, and "casting accounts." He was neither studious nor teachable. As a boy he preferred sport to study, and as a man he chose to rely on his own fertile ideas rather than to accept guidance from others.

The log cabin school that he attended stood in a grove of scrub pines.

It is said that he was chosen to read the Declaration of Independence when a copy of the document first reached Waxhaw in the summer of 1776. Perhaps he was, but it seems odd that such an important task should be assigned to a boy not yet ten.

He grew up amidst a rough people whose tastes ran strongly to horse-racing, cockfighting, and heavy drinking, and whose ideal of excellence found expression in a readiness to fight upon any and all occasions in defense of what they considered to be their personal honor.

It is clear that he was a mischievous, high-spirited boy, and often got into trouble. At least one anecdote is thoroughly in keeping with his career in manhood. Some of his playmates, so the story goes, once loaded a gun to the muzzle and gave it to him to fire. As they expected, it kicked him over, but they missed the fun they looked for. He sprang to his feet white with rage, and exclaimed, with an oath, "If one of you laughs, I'll kill him!"— and no one laughed.

The boy got little education, and never was a scholar. He wrote the English language with difficulty, making many errors of grammar and spelling, and spoke it with many peculiarities of pronunciation. Of other languages he knew nothing; of the great body of science, literature, and the arts he knew next to nothing.

The Revolutionary War interrupted his schooling, but it gave home to a different kind of education.

During the American Revolutionary War, he acted as a courier. He was captured, at age thirteen, and mistreated by his British captors.

He and his brother were released through the efforts of their mother, who brought about an exchange of prisoners.

But his brother died from smallpox before his release. His mother stayed on in the prison camp to care for the sick soldiers, until she succumbed to the cholera.

He was thus left an orphan, weakened in body by the smallpox, which he took while he was in prison. Moreover, he bore on his head the mark of a blow from the sword of a British officer whose boots he had refused to polish.

As an orphan, he adapted to shifting circumstances and cultivated the powerful. It does not appear that during the next seven years, while he was growing to manhood, he gave himself with much industry either to study or to work. For six months he was employed in the shop of a saddler, but he seems to have learned more about filling saddles than about making them, for he became somewhat famous as a horseman even in a country where the love of horseflesh was universal.

The uncle with whom he now lived was a serious-minded man who by his industry had won means ample for the comfortable subsistence of his enlarged household.

In his early teens he swore like a trooper, chewed tobacco incessantly, acquired a taste for strong drink, and set a pace for wildness which few of his associates could keep up.

He was passionately fond of running foot races, leaping the bar, jumping, wrestling, and every sort of sport that partook of the character of mimic battle—and he never acknowledged defeat.

He longed to see the rest of this new country. Over and over he listened to the stories that passing travelers would tell about what lay to the south and north.

It was exciting for him to think that he was a character in a story about a country that seemed to have so much promise.

He took an apprenticeship with a man named Joseph White, a saddler. He not only learned how to make saddles, but he also came into contact with men who knew a horse's importance, both as a practical tool and as a status symbol.
He was an angry young man.

- eight -

He was the first president to be born a citizen of the United States of America.

He was literally born to the bosom of politics, for his father's tavern doubled as the local polling place at election time, on December 5, 1782.

From his cradle he was of the non-committal tribe. He had always two ways to do a thing.

Both of his parents were exclusively of Dutch descent, their ancestors being among the most respectable of those emigrants from Holland who established themselves in the earliest period of our colonial history in the ancient settlement of Kinderhook.

His parents were humble, plain, and not much troubled with book knowledge.

His mother was a woman remarkable for her good sense and agreeable manners.

His father was a farmer in moderate circumstances, an upright and an intelligent man, whose virtuous conduct and amiable temper enabled him (as such qualities are apt to do) to pass through a long life, almost without contention or controversy.

He had two full brothers, and two full sisters.

For all his parents' economies, they struggled for their meager existence.

In his own words, he possessed "an uncommonly active mind" and he was sent to the local one-room schoolhouse. But owing to his father's pecuniary embarrassment, he left school at thirteen. An acute consciousness of what he gave up pervades his writing. In his autobiography he bemoans his lack of reading.

It was in the log cabin school of the village that he learned to read and to write.

He studied later at Kinderhook Academy, one of the higher schools which in New York have done good work, though not equaling the like of schools in Massachusetts. There, he learned a little Latin.

What little education he got, he got it honestly, and always behaved himself with great propriety, never being accused of taking anything secretly from his school-mates. While others were breaking open trunks, and stealing their comrades' money, nothing of that kind was ever brought to his charge.

If the decision to leave school cost him something, it also brought him closer to the political world that fascinated him.

The remainder of his education is self-taught, and as he pored, night after night, after his long day's work was done, over his hard lesson — hard because he had none to assist him — he early gave evidence of that perseverance and industry which has so eminently distinguished him in later life.

But when at fourteen years of age he entered a law office, he had of course the chief discipline of book-learning still to acquire.

Preparing for the law and studying in the same office were several young men of wealthy parents, and numerous were the jokes and sneers which were cast upon the "Dutch Boy," as they, in derision, called him; and many were the wonders of these wiseacres, when the subject of this would pass an examination. To them it seemed an impossibility that he who made so little pretention, and who was compelled so many hours during the day to labor for a subsistence, could ever master the intricacies of the law; they little knew the many hours of laborious study which were taken from the time usually allotted to rest, and still less did they know the indomitable spirit of the friendless boy, the object of their sneering sarcasms.

He always regretted that he hadn't read more in his youth. "Instead of laying up stores of useful knowledge," he said. "I read for amusement."

The warm and friendly atmosphere of his family's tavern helped to shape his outlook on life. Although his parents had little money for material things, they gave him the chance to mix with people of various backgrounds and professions. He enjoyed the atmosphere immensely. Working alongside his father, he met well-known statesmen, politicians, and lawyers who treated him as an adult. Alexander Hamilton and Aaron Burr were among those who frequented the tavern and stirred his interest in politics during his early years.

While studying law, he did a variety of helpful jobs, including careful copying of legal notes. He soon became known as the "boy lawyer."

Even as a young man he knew how to disagree without being disagreeable.

He liked to dress in stylish, expensive clothes. He borrowed money to pay for a tri-cornered hat, knee breeches, and buckled shoes that were in style at the time. Some called him a dandy and criticized him for trying to be someone he was not.

He early showed a zeal in his law studies as well as an interest in public affairs and a fondness for extemporaneous debate, with the result that he was only eighteen when he was chosen to sit in a local nominating convention.

He was admitted to the bar (profession of lawyers) in 1803 at the age of twenty-one.

- nine -

He was born of the blood and bred
in the school of the patriots of the
Revolution, the last American President
born as a British subject.

He came into the world on the 9th day of February, 1773, on
his family's plantation at a place called Berkley, on the James
River, about 25 miles below Richmond, in Charles City County,
Virginia.

His father was one of the earliest and most conspicuous patriots
of the Revolution, a delegate to the Continental Congress.

His mother was a relative of Martha Washington.

The child may look back with conscious pride, to the whole life
of his father, but he must still depend upon his own exertions,
his own acts, and his own genius, for any distinction shown to
himself.

His house was a red-brick mansion on a green lawn, with a
porch shading the back of the house where the avenue came up
from the pike.

In the summer of 1780, when he was seven years old, the
colonies still seemed far away from victory. War was his favorite
game to play when he was a boy.

He saved his sister Sally from drowning when she fell off a
barge they were playing on. He clutched her dress and helped
her swing one leg up and over the side of the barge. When he
saw that she wasn't breathing, he slapped her on the back. That
did no good, so he stepped astride his sister and lifted her from

the waist. His arms ached but he held her and shook her until she sputtered and gasped and coughed up water. Then he let her down gently. She said to him, You saved my life. His heart was pounding, but he was pleased that he had not been too scared to act when his sister needed his help.

He had unblemished skin, silky brown hair, a long nose, and a long, thin face. He embodied a familiar kind of young Southerner: Slender, graceful, and a bit delicate in build.

He was the youngest of seven children, which under the laws and customs of the day limited his prospects. It was plain to him early in life that he would have to learn self-sufficiency. It was equally plain that he was ambitious.

He entered upon his education after his elder brothers had finished theirs. At the age of fourteen, he entered the Presbyterian Hampden–Sydney College. He attended the school until 1790, becoming well-versed in Latin and basic French. He was removed by his Episcopalian father, possibly because of a religious revival occurring at the school.

He briefly attended a boys' academy in Southampton County. He allegedly was influenced by anti-slavery Quakers and Methodists at the school. Angered, his pro-slavery father had him transfer to Philadelphia, Pennsylvania, for medical training.

He entered the University of Pennsylvania in 1790, where he studied medicine under Dr. Benjamin Rush. As he later told his biographer, he did not enjoy the subject. Shortly after he started these studies, his father died, leaving him without funds for further schooling. Eighteen years old, he abandoned the study of medicine.

He had a mobile, expressive mouth with a humorous curl to the lips. He looked like a young man who might have been amusing company. Scattered sources from his early years seem to support this. He had "much resource in conversation," according to a man who met him when he was twenty.

After the death of his mother in 1793, he inherited a portion of the family's estate, including about 3,000 acres of land and several slaves. Still in the army at the time, he sold his land to his brother.

A long letter he wrote at age twenty-one to his older brother likewise suggests good humor and wit: He wrote in the smooth, easy style of Henry Fielding or Laurence Sterne, with graceful transitions and clever turns of phrase.

Before long, the hostilities of the Indians in the Northwest began to awaken public solicitude, and he felt irresistibly impelled to relinquish his professional pursuits in order to dedicate his life to the defense of his country.

In 1795 at the age of twenty-two, he met Anna Tuthill Symmes, of North Bend, Ohio. She was a daughter of Judge John Cleves Symmes, a prominent figure in the state and former representative to the Congress of the Confederation. When he asked the judge for permission to marry Anna, he was refused. He and Anna waited until Judge Symmes left town on business, then they eloped.

- ten -

He was born—on March 29, 1790—to wealth and privilege in one of Virginia's first families.

He was the sixth of eventually eight children.

He was raised on a slave plantation as a member of the political elite and social aristocracy of his state and nation. His father was a member of the Revolutionary generation and a friend to the leading founding fathers, including Thomas Jefferson.

Little is known of his early years (most of his personal papers were destroyed during the Civil War). His childhood and youth are largely veiled in obscurity, with almost an entire absence of the myths with which tradition usually fills in the gaps in the careers of noted men.

It is unfortunate that there are no apocryphal stories interwoven with the brief narrative of his youth, for no opportunity is afforded his biographers of exercising their skill in debunking the accepted account of his early life.

It is more than likely, however, that his boyhood was not substantially different from that of other young scions of the Tidewater aristocracy of that day.

His youth was spent on a 1200-acre estate—a plantation called Greenway because "its grass doth grown so green"—lying along the north side of the James River. There, under a large willow tree, his father often played the fiddle and told stories of the Revolutionary War to his children and the children of his slaves.

He loved music and he began to play the fiddle at an early age. As a boy and as a young man, he learned the values and social graces expected of a Virginia gentleman.

The greatest misfortune of his childhood was the death of his mother.

She died when he was seven years old. Friends of his believed him to be much like his mother: soft-spoken and gentle-mannered.

Of one thing we may be sure—that he unconsciously imbibed many of the prejudices and convictions of a father whose personality was characterized by rugged individuality and whose patriotism was deeply tinged with localism.

During the early years of his life, he exhibited very few, if any, characteristics that gave promise of extraordinary eminence in the future.

He seems never to have sown any wild oats. He was a youth who accepted without question or protest the social ideals of his day.

His father was a judge, known for his strong convictions and prejudices both of which he expressed with utter fearlessness.

It is true that he was precocious and very good-looking, but these traits do not always augur exceptional success in later life.

As a schoolboy he had a slender frame, a very prominent thin roman nose, silky brown hair, a bright blue eye, a merry mischievous smile and silvery laugh.

His personality apparently embodied more of the gentle virtues of his mother than the stern qualities of his father. So amiable and docile was he as a child that an overanxious parent might have feared a leaning toward effeminacy.

However weak his body, he excelled at school. Ancient history, poetry, and the works of William Shakespeare were his favorite subjects. He learned Latin and Greek and found Adam Smith's *Wealth of Nations*, with its call for trade unrestricted by tariffs or government interference, consistent with his emerging political philosophy.

In early boyhood he attended the small school kept by John McMurdo, who was so diligent in his use of the birch that it is a wonder he did not whip all the sense out of his scholars.

At the age of eleven he was one of the ring-leaders in a rebellion in which the despotic McMurdo was overpowered by numbers, tied hand and foot, and left locked up in the schoolhouse until late at night, when a passing traveler effected an entrance and released him.

His education in republicanism was fostered in 1802 when, as a twelve year old, he prepared to enter the college of William and Mary. It was a natural choice; both his grandfather and father, like most Southern patricians, had gone there, as had Thomas Jefferson.

Those who knew him at college described him as a quiet, serious boy who preferred writing poetry and playing the violin to the rough-and-tumble. Physically, he was very slight…his long, thin patrician face dominated by the high cheekbones and prominent nose. His lips were thin and tight, his dark brown hair was silken. Illnesses—intestinal pain and chronic diarrhea or respiratory ailments—were his constant companions. He memorized passages from Adam Smith's writings.

Educated at William and Mary in Bishop James Madison's school of empire and national destiny, he had been groomed to assume as his birthright a career dedicated to public service and political leadership. Like his father before him, he found his calling in public service.

He graduated from William and Mary in 1~~907~~ 1807, a few months after his seventeenth birthday. He was one of four students selected to deliver his class's commencement address.

He finished his legal studies in two years, at age nineteen. Although he had not yet reached the age required for admission

38

to the bar, he was admitted, no doubt because of his excellent record and family connections.

He quickly made a name for himself and a comfortable living as an attorney specializing in criminal law.

He chose the law because, he said, it was "the high road to fame."

- eleven -

He was born on November 2, 1795 in Mecklenburg County, North Carolina.

He was the first of ten children.

His father was a slaveholder, successful farmer, and surveyor of Scots-Irish descent. His mother, Jane Polk (née Knox), was a descendant of a brother of the Scottish religious reformer John Knox.

His ancestors came to North America in the seventeenth century from Scotland and Ireland, and their search for farmland took them to Pennsylvania and Maryland before they settled on the North Carolina frontier.

The American Revolution brought new prosperity to his family, including land warrants (options to purchase) in the future state of Tennessee.

As a young man, his frailty prevented him from participating in the rigors of frontier life. He spent much of his childhood at home, where his mother instilled in him her Presbyterian faith and taught him to cope with his physical shortcomings through rigid self-discipline. As a result, he learned at an early age to control his emotions.

His schooling had been marginal, in large part because of his rather poor health. He was decidedly frail.

He assisted his father in the management of his farm, and was his almost constant companion in his surveying excursions.

In 1812 he survived surgery for urinary stones.

Resting uncomfortably on a makeshift bed in a covered wagon, he bounced along as the eight-hundred-mile journey to Philadelphia to receive the care of Dr. Philip Syng Physick, later known as "the father of American surgery," began. But before traveling very far into Kentucky, he "was seized by a paroxysm more painful than any that had preceded it." Doubting that he could survive all the way to Philadelphia, his family turned to Dr. Ephraim McDowell of Danville, Kentucky who—relatively speaking—was also a surgeon of some note. Relying on a liberal does of brandy as both anesthetic and antisepsis, Dr. McDowell made an incision behind his scrotum and forced a sharp, pointed instrument called a gorget through his prostate and into his bladder and removed the urinary stones with a forceps.

Outwardly he appeared no worse for the wear.

Had he possessed a strong physique, doubtless he would have shared the fate of the average eldest son and have been trained to cultivate the family estate. But he was not strong and his first years in Tennessee were spent in making good use of such limited educational advantages as were afforded in a pioneer community.

He was studious and ambitious, but fate seemed determined to deprive him of the opportunity for satisfying his desire for an education.

His father, believing that a more active life than that of a student would be conducive to health, determined to make a business man of his son. Accordingly, much to his disgust and protest, he was placed with a merchant to learn the business. After remaining but a few weeks with the merchant, however, his earnest appeals to come home overcame the resistance of his father, and in July, 1813, he was permitted to resume his education under the guidance of Reverend Robert Henderson at a small academy near Columbia, Tennessee. For about a year he "read the usual course of Latin authors, part of the Greek testament and a few of the dialogues of Lucian," and, according to the testimony of his preceptor, he was diligent in his studies, and his moral conduct was unexceptionable and exemplary.

His scholarly inclinations led him to the local Zion Church Academy and then to the Bradley Academy in Murfreesboro.

After passing the entrance exams with high scores, he began his college career as a sophomore in January 1816 at the University of North Carolina at Chapel Hill. Two and one-half years later he graduated with honors in mathematics and the classics.

At college he manifested those peculiar traits which later characterized his career as a statesman. Eschewing the less profitable, but usually more attractive, side of college life, his time was occupied with hard and well directed study.

His ambition to excel, wrote one of his political friends, was equaled by his perseverance alone, in proof of which it is said he never missed a recitation nor omitted the punctilious performance of any duty.

Neither at college nor at a later time did he ever deceive himself or attempt to deceive others by assuming great native brilliancy. He never posed as one whose genius made it easy for him to decide great questions offhand. He never attempted to conceal the fact that his conclusions were reached as the result of unremitting labor. And if his conclusions were sometimes attacked as unsound, he was, on the other hand, spared the embarrassment of ridicule, which often fell to the lot of his more brilliant competitors during his long political career.

So carefully he avoided the pedantry of classical display, which is the false taste of our day and country, as almost to hire his acquisitions which distinguished his early career. His preference for the useful and substantial, indicated by his youthful passion for mathematics, has made him select a style of elocution, which would perhaps be deemed too plain by shallow admirers of flashy declamation.

His most valuable education may have come from membership in one of the university's two literary societies. He joined the Dialectic Society during his first term at Chapel Hill and was soon engrossed in its weekly debates and essay presentations. It was here that he learned to speak, write, and formulate an argument.

He was punctual and prompt in every exercise, and never absent from recitation of any religious services of the institution.

He well understood the difference between true merit and pretense. Untiring assiduity and close application characterized him throughout his whole collegiate course.

The lessons that he learned in school were never forgotten. Of his classical training he retained the substantial and discarded the ornate.

- twelve -

He was born in Virginia (in 1784) but raised in Kentucky.

He grew up in an isolated home on the Muddy Fork of Beargrass Creek.

He came from a distinguished family with large estates and a long history of public service. His father had served as an officer in the Continental Army during the Revolutionary War.

Little is known about his childhood at all. He had some formal education from tutors, but his spelling, grammar, and handwriting skills were considered weak.

Although there were no other houses in sight, his childhood wasn't lonely. He had a friend named George who lived on the farm next-door.

His cousins lived about eighty miles away in Louisville.

His first tutor was a traveling schoolteacher from Connecticut who rode between New England and the frontier on his mule, setting up school wherever he happened to be. His second tutor was a more accomplished scholar from Ireland.

He never betrayed a yearning for book learning.

Like other children on the frontier, he spent much of his time learning practical things by helping to clear the land and manage a quickly growing plantation. He also learned to face danger. Wolves and wildcats roamed the forests around his farm.

His nursery tales were stories of Indian butchery which had but recently been perpetrated upon the neighbors of his parents;

and as he grew larger, he often heard the shriek of the maiden and innocent, the sharp crack of the rifle that announced their death, and then the fierce conflict between the father and his savage foe.

He learned to barricade his own door, and spend the night in watchful intensity.

At the age of six years, he was placed at school, under the direction of a Mr. Ayers. Even here he was in continual danger of the tomahawk, and many of the larger scholars were obliged to go armed. While here, he became distinguished among his companions for his activity, decision and bluntness of character, modesty of demeanor, and general intelligence. These are shining qualities in a school-boy, and he soon became the acknowledged and general favorite of a large portion of his comrades.

From a child, his mind possessed a keen relish for military narratives, and in youth he began to long for an opportunity to display himself in the field.

He had mental qualities of thoughtfulness, judgment, shrewdness, and stability, not often found united in youth. But a peculiar trait of his character, and one not often connected with a sanguine temperament, was firmness.

Original obscurity or early trials could not have shadowed his genius or repressed his energies.

Among the anecdotes current in Kentucky respecting his childhood, is one of his watching at home with his brother, and casting bullets, while his father was out engaged with the Indians.

His boyhood was distinguished by indications of straightforward, manly independence of character, inflexibility of purpose, frank and open disposition, foresight, decision and energy, modest and retiring demeanor, and thoughtful, inquiring mind, that saw him borne triumphantly through difficulties and dangers before which men educated in a less severe school would have shrunk in despair.

Many family and neighborhood anecdotes are told to illustrate his daring and adventurous character, and his love for dangerous enterprises. Night after night he was in the habit of seeing the house barricaded, and the arms prepared to repel any attack that might be made before morning dawned. Scarcely a week passed that there was not an alarm, or an actual incursion of Indians amongst the settlements. Even on his way to school he was in danger of the tomahawk and scalping knife.

He was reared by his father to his own profession—that of a farmer; and, until his majority, was practically engaged in it, working with his own hands, and laying the foundation of robust health, hardy habits, and persevering industry.

He took great delight in fishing and hunting and was often absent, roaming through forests and over boundless prairies, for days and nights together, in quest of game.

When he was seventeen years old he swam across the Ohio River, from the Kentucky to the Indian shore, in the month of March when the river was filled with floating ice, which is a feat far surpassing in danger and difficulty the far-famed exploit of swimming Hellespont.

No obstacle would dampen his indomitable energy, or discourage him from attempting the most hazardous enterprises.

Upon leaving school he continued the exercise of those sports and labors which suited the ardor of his temperament. He often performed feats of strength and difficulty which would excite the wonder and applause of friends, and rivalry of others.

He applied for a commission in the army, and, by the aid of his powerful family connections, his application was successful; and on the 3rd of May, 1808, he received a commission as first lieutenant in the Seventh Regiment of the United States Infantry.

His first extant letter, in which he accepted his commission in the United States Army, was rough and full of misspellings.

He had a great fondness for military life, even before he commenced a course of rigid tactical instruction. He could often be seen with his comrades practicing the different evolutions of a company drill, with as much gravity and emulation as though under orders before an enemy.

He was also, like his father, a shrewd businessman and competent farmer.

His young ambition was not satisfied, and a wide field opened before him for the gratification of his long indulged and ardent aspirations for military fame.

Though he was a planter, he was first and foremost a soldier. He was not attracted to fancy uniforms nor to the parade ground, but practical soldiering seems to have become second nature to him.

- thirteen -

He was born on January 7, 1800 in a log cabin in Cayuga County, New York, which was then part of the western frontier of the new nation.

He was born in poverty, poorly schooled as a child, and largely self-educated after that.

His unusual first name was his mother's maiden name, a common practice among New Englanders, which his family had been until 1799, when they gave up on farming the rocky soil of Vermont in the belief that central New York offered better land and more opportunity.

Not long after his birth, his family lost their home and the land on which it stood and moved to the Finger Lakes region of upstate New York.

His family homestead was part of almost two million acres of New York land known as the Military Tract. His family were tenant farmers, otherwise known as sharecroppers.

He was assigned chores even as a toddler. As he grew older, he took on more and more work. Much of it was labor that required a bent back and strong arms—he hoed corn, moved hay with the curved blade of a scythe, and reaped wheat. In springtime he prepared the soil for planting with a wooden plow that was pulled by a mule when one was handy. When a mule was nowhere to be found, he plowed the soil himself. In the winter he chopped wood for the fireplace.

In his early childhood, he possessed a sedate gravity of manners and a peaceful quietude that was extraordinary in a child of his age.

When he was nine he received a certificate from school for spelling 224 words without missing one.

The first novel he read was the *Voyages and Adventures of Captain Robert Boyle*.

When he did not feel like working, he would steal away to hunt rabbits with his father's rifle or settle under a tree on the banks of the Skaneateles Lake, cast a line for fish, and doze. His father lectured him on the evils of idleness.

Early he learned to hoe corn, mow hay, and reap wheat. As he grew older, the wooden plow became a familiar implement in his hand. By the time he had reached the age of fifteen he had mastered most of the primitive, frontier farming skills.

Possessing little in common with other children, for the amusements incident to that age, he was rarely seen engaged in sports which were a source of enjoyment to the other boys. He loved his young associates, but had no desire to participate in their frolicsome pastimes. The quality of his disposition was steady and earnest, yet mild and gentle.

He was never known to quarrel with other boys, or to use language in the least exceptional to anyone.

In personal appearance, at this time, he is described to have been rather slim, with his proportions undeveloped, and exceedingly awkward in his movements.

Hard work made him a sturdy youth. He was apprenticed to learn the business of carding wool and dressing cloth. It was an unhappy apprenticeship for him. His employer was an impatient and demanding man with a brutal streak, who threatened to strike him when his fingers were not nimble enough on the cloth. In retaliation, he picked up a small ax and threatened his employer. Three months later, he borrowed $30 and paid off his obligation to the cloth maker. Now free, he walked one hundred miles back to his family.

Still, his father again arranged for him to be apprenticed to a cloth-processing establishment near the village of New Hope. Once more, living far from home, it was a lonely life for him.

These apprenticeships made him "feel for the weak and unprotected, and to hate the insolent tyrant in every station of life."

During the months of attending the mill machines, he became painfully aware of his ignorance.

He was fifteen years when his real education began, as he started to steal and borrow books. As a child, he had been taught how to read, but aside from the family's King James Bible, he had little opportunity to do so. He knew virtually nothing about grammar or how to phrase things correctly—skills that he would need desperately in his future life in politics.

Here, as the years passed, he grew from boy to man.

In his teens and determined to improve himself, he bought a small dictionary and began memorizing words to enlarge his vocabulary. Sometimes he would secretly glance at the dictionary while carding wool and silently work out the pronunciation for words to himself.

When he was seventeen years old, he heard about a small library that offered to loan books to the public. He joined and soon was reading eagerly.

Voraciously he attacked books. No method plotted the course of his reading; it was aimless, but extensive. Immediately one lesson emerged: He recognized the woeful limitations of his vocabulary.

Eventually, he found himself drawn to books dealing with

history, government, and law.

Roughly two years later a private academy was established in New Hope. Recognizing the need to improve his education, he enrolled while still apprenticing at the cloth-processing establishment. The school was coeducational, and for the first time he came into close social contact with females other than his sisters. One of them was Abigail Powers, who would one day become his wife.

Though a pale replica of eastern models, the school surpassed anything he had known. He gloried in the experience. For the first time he heard a sentence parsed, for the first time he saw a map, and for the first time he began to experience the pleasures of female society.

He had for some time conceived the idea of reading law, a profession for which he seemed naturally to have entertained a strong predilection.

During the spring and summer of 1818, he prosecuted his business with his employer in his former double capacity of master workman and bookkeeper. During that fall, so ardent had become his desire to engage in the study of the law, without hindrance imposed by the duties of his trade, that he ventured to communicate them to his father. It was about this time he attracted the notice of Judge Wood, a lawyer of estimable worth, residing at no great distance from his father's, who persuaded him to devote his studies to the law.

- fourteen -

He was born on November 23, 1804, in Hillsborough, New Hampshire.

His ancestors were all plain, honest, and intelligent Democrats, fond of serving their country in time of war on the field of battle—in time of peace as loyal citizens.

He would later describe his mother as affectionate and endlessly forgiving of his youthful hijinks, but it was his far sterner father, the most influential man in Hillsborough County, who had the greater impact on him.

His father had enlisted at seventeen years old in the armies of his country, during the Revolutionary struggle, when the meagre band of oppressed patriots were contending for civil and religious liberty against the trained vassals sent by British power and rapacity to subjugate her struggling colony.

Here he is: short, stout, rosy-faced, with a great head. Where he goes the other children go; what he does, they do. Already a little world has begun to follow him. Look at him as he runs around among the candle molds, talking like a philosopher. Does he seem likely to stand in the French court amid the splendors of the palace of Versailles, the most popular and conspicuous person among all the jeweled multitude who fill the mirrored, the golden, the blazing halls except the king himself? Does he look as though he would one day ask the French king for an army to help establish the independence of his country, and that the throne would bow to him?

He was hardly a bookish youth. He loved the outdoors and enjoyed roughhousing, swimming, fishing, and ice skating far more than lessons in school.

He developed a curious liking for a trumpet and a gun. He liked to march about to noise, and this noise he was pleased to make himself—to blow his own trumpet.

Even as a boy he evinced the personal charm that would smooth his political rise. He was his playmates' ringleader, and adults, especially adult women, found him an altogether winning lad—honest, polite, and poised. To put it differently—perhaps more ominously—from boyhood on he was eager to please other people.

When he was a child, at seven years old, his friends, on a holiday, filled his pockets with coppers. He went directly to a shop where they sold toys for children, and, being charmed with the sound of a whistle that he met by the way in the hands of another boy, he voluntarily offered him all his money for one. He then went home, and went whistling all over the house, much pleased with his whistle, but disturbing all his family. His brothers and sisters and cousins, understanding the bargain he had made, told him he had given four times as much for it as the whistle was worth. This put him in mind what good things he might have bought with the rest of the money; and they laughed at him so much for his folly that he cried with vexation, and the reflection gave him more chagrin than the whistle gave him pleasure. This, however, was afterward of use to him, the impression continuing on in his mind; so that often, when he was tempted to buy some unnecessary thing, he said to himself, "Don't give too much for the whistle, and so he saved his money."

He did not like school, but his father, who lacked a formal education of his own, was determined that his sons attend college. Thus he was dispatched to a series of academies outside of Hillsborough to learn Latin and Greek in preparation for the required college entrance exams.

His frank manners, his generous disposition, endeared him to all his associates, and it is a significant fact, that his juvenile popularity is not diminished by lapse of time.

The old people of his neighborhood give a very delightful picture of him at this early age. They describe him as a beautiful boy, with blue eyes, light curling hair, and a sweet expression of face. The traits presented of him indicate moral symmetry, kindliness, and a delicate texture of sentiment, rather than marked prominences of character. His instructors testify to his propriety of conduct, his fellow-pupils to his sweetness of disposition and cordial sympathy.

He was then a youth, with the boy and man in him, vivacious, mirthful, slender, of a fair complexion, with light hair that had a curl in it: his bright and cheerful aspect made a kind of sunshine, both as regarded its radiance and its warmth; insomuch that no shyness of disposition, in his associates, could well resist its influence.

He had all the advantages that come to the son of a distinguished parent.

For several years he attended school in the neighboring towns of Hancock and Francestown. He left Francestown for Exeter Academy, where he completed his preparatory studies, and entered Bowdoin College at the precocious age of sixteen, in the year 1820.

Among his classmates he was extremely popular.

At Bowdoin, he became most intimate with Nathaniel Hawthorne, and in his circle of friends were the poet Henry Wadsworth Longfellow and John P. Hale.

In the dormitory at night, when solitary study was the prescribed regimen, he was famous for bursting into other students' rooms to start furniture-smashing wrestling matches. Wrestling was not his only nighttime activity in those first years at Bowdoin. In violation of the school's rules, he and his closest pals snuck out of the dorm to frequent a Brunswick tavern.

Heavy drinking and his name go together like a horse and

carriage.

As a result of his carefree behavior, he ranked dead last academically in his class by the end of his sophomore year at Bowdoin.

While at Bowdoin, he honed his public speaking, which made him a natural for the legal profession.

There is little else that it is worthwhile to relate, as regards his college course, unless it be, that, during one of his winter vacations, he taught a country school. So many of the statesmen of New England, like him, have performed their first public service in the character of pedagogue, that it seems almost a necessary step on the ladder of advancement.

- fifteen -

Born on April 23, 1791, he was the second of eleven children.

He was born in a log cabin at Cove Gap in Pennsylvania. Sadly, three of his siblings died in infancy, leaving him with four sisters and three brothers as he grew up.

In an unfinished autobiography, he described his father as having great force of character, but he credited his mother for any distinction that he had attained.

Surrounded by younger sisters and an adoring mother who quoted Milton and Shakespeare to her children and engaged them in discussions about public affairs, he occupied a privileged but challenging position in his family.

He was, by all accounts, including his own, an excellent student.

His father was a wealthy merchant and farmer who emigrated from Donegal in Ireland in 1783.

Not long after he was born, his sister Mary died. But his family continued to grow.

When he was six, his family moved to a spacious two-story home in Mercersburg. For the first time, he had playmates other than his sisters. He started school at the Old Stone Academy. As at other schools of the time, he and his classmates were soon learning to read Latin as well as English.

His early years at Stony Batter and in Mercersburg gave him a lasting love for the countryside and the slow pace of village life.

By the time he was eleven, he had four sisters. And four brothers were born later, two of them after he left home.

His family's trading post was located right next to a gap in the Allegheny Mountains of Western Pennsylvania.

As a boy and the oldest child, he was expected to spend many hours a week helping out in the family store. He learned the value of hard work and thrift from his father, who had been an orphan in Ireland and was determined to make a better life for his family.

His father taught him to pay close attention to business and to remember details. He loved his father, and he worked hard to impress him. His father was stern and made him work hard.

His father had taught him to be the store's record keeper. In this job, he wrote down the prices of everything that came into the store (how much the store paid for goods) and the prices of everything that went out (how much the customers paid). At the end of each month, he added up those numbers to see how much money the store had made.

He closed one eye and concentrated hard on the handwritten pages in front of him. He was nine years old and perched on a stool behind the counter at his father's general store in Mercersburg, Pennsylvania.

His mother taught him the elements of her deeply held Presbyterian faith. He also learned from her how to deal with misfortunes calmly and methodically. His mother was less strict. His mother did not have much education, but she loved to read.

He also learned a lot from the local farmers who came to his father's store. From behind the counter, he heard these men discussing politics. He learned about the two prominent political parties of the day.

At his father's store, he developed sympathy for the rural, farming lifestyle of the customers.

He was influenced by following his father's business affairs. He learned the importance of keeping good records, and trained himself to have good handwriting.

Like many boys, he did not always get along with his father. His father would sometimes give him jobs too difficult for him to complete and then would criticize him when they weren't done properly. He rarely received praise from his father, no matter how well he did. He loved and respected his father, but he longed for his approval.

At first he studied hard and obeyed all the rules, but this won him few friends. "To be a sober, plodding, industrious youth was to incur the ridicule of the mass of the students," he later recalled. He began to join the other students in breaking the rules and defying their teachers, but he continued to be a good student.

As he approached the end of his schooling, he and his parents began to discuss his further education. His mother wanted him to become a minister. His father suggested that a career in law might be more suitable. As the oldest son in a large family, he might one day need to help provide for his sisters and brother, which would be difficult on a minister's income.

Then he was expelled from school due to bad behavior. His father was disappointed.

He promised the school that he would change his ways, and he was readmitted. He focused on his studies and made excellent grades.

He made good on his promise to behave better. He excelled at his schoolwork. Some of his professors came to think of him as a conceited young man, who was mostly interested in impressing others with his intelligence.

His grades qualified him to be one of two students in the class to graduate with honors, but the faculty refused to consider him. He still had a reputation as a troublemaker, and he had shown little respect for his teachers. He was furious, and some of his classmates supported him. His father, on the other hand, urged him to accept the decision like a man. Before graduation, the school leaders compromised: They allowed him to give a speech at graduation ceremonies but still refused to award him honors. The experience helped him learn to deal with setbacks in a mature way.

He graduated from Dickinson College in Carlisle at age 18, in spite of being expelled a year earlier for bad behavior.
After graduating he went on to study law at Lancaster. He read legal books and documents all day. Then in the early evening, he would take long walks, thinking about everything he had read and repeating it to himself out loud. He was admitted to the bar in 1812.

- sixteen -

It cannot be too often stated that cheerful friendliness was the most striking feature of his personality.

He helped his father all he could.

He ate what was set before him, making no complaint. He did try to show off sometimes. But he was a good boy.

He was born in on the 12th of February, 1809 at Sinking Springs, near Hodgenville, Kentucky. He was born in a log cabin that was eighteen feet long and sixteen feet wide. The door to the cabin swung open and shut on leather hinges, and a tiny window looked out on his world. His bed was made from corn husks, his covers, skins from bears.

When he was two, his folks packed their few goods, moved to Knob Creek. The Cumberland Trail ran close to their new cabin, so he saw peddlers, pioneers, politicians, traders, and slaves pass by. As he grew, he talked to travelers—heard where they'd been, where they were going. He saw the word was wider than his own. His ideas stretched. His questions rose. His dreams were stirred.

His father was a hardworking man who made a reputation for himself through sheer hard work. His father soon became one of the richest men in the county. However, everything went downhill in 1816, when his father lost all his property in various court cases.

He seemed to grow bigger every day. By the time he was seven, he was tall as his sister, though she was two years older.

When he was only nine years old, his mother died after suffering from milk sickness. There is no evidence that his emotions were unlike those of other children of similar age in the same situation. His older sister took care of him until their father remarried a year later.

He was notably studious in everything.

He learned to plow a straight furrow. He put seeds in the furrows.

A schoolmate tells us that he was 'long and tall...wore low shoes, short socks and his britches made of buckskin' that were so short that they left 'bare and naked more than six or more inches of his shin bone'.

He did all the writing for the family and indeed for everybody in the settlement. Even more important to his avid mind was the fact that he learned to read with ease and fluency.

The farm boys in their evenings at Jones's store in Gentryville talked about how he was always reading, digging into books, stretching out flat on his stomach in front of the fireplace, studying till midnight and past midnight, picking a piece of charcoal to write on the fire shovel, shaving off what he wrote, and then writing more—till midnight and past midnight. The next thing, he would be reading books between plow handles.

After he had learned to read, he poured into the ears of companions everything he read.

He liked to explain to other people what he was getting from books; explaining an idea to someone else made it clearer to him. The habit was growing on him of reading out loud; words came more real if picked from the silent page of the book and pronounced on the tongue; new balances and values of words stood out if spoken aloud.

In the Indiana schools he excelled, it appears, particularly in spelling and could "spell down" the whole class when, at the close of the school week every Friday, the children were placed in line against the log wall for a contest in spelling. He was unselfish with his proficiency. He was good at figuring, and had the best handwriting of anyone at school.

Including the two schools in Kentucky, he went to school for less than a year.

When at home he ciphered on boards when he had no paper or no slate. When the board would get too black, he would shave it off with a drawing knife and go on again. When he had paper, he put his sums down on it. He made a copybook by sewing together blanks sheets. In this he did his work in arithmetic.

He early showed kindness of heart which distinguished him throughout his life. One day he found some of the boys being cruel to a terrapin, or turtle. He made them stop. He reproved the children for their cruelty to an animal, particularly placing glowing coals on the backs of turtles. Then he wrote a composition in which he said that animals had feelings the same as folks.

He would carry a book with him when he had to go to work, and over its pages he would pore when rest time came. He was always reading, scribbling, writing, ciphering, writing poetry. The books at home exhausted, he ranged the countryside in search of more, an intellectual prowler for sustenance of the printed page. People from miles around loaned him books.

He naturally assumed the leadership of the boys. But he was never dogmatic, it appears, never aggressive in his views, never turbulent or offensive in stating them, never insistent that others should think as he thought.

He was not very fond of girls. The girls liked him, however, because he was friendly, somewhat sociable.

He did not like what he called "fizzlegigs and fireworks."

By the time he was fourteen he was as tall as his father.

He began making speeches as early as his fifteenth year. He would mount a tree stump, or stand a fence and talk to his fellow workers, who would leave their jobs in fields or woods to listen. For he never bored anybody.

The clearness and simplicity of these youthful speeches, so striking that all made note of and remembered those qualities, were partly the result of his writing and rewriting what he read and thought.

He was abnormally gregarious and, when not lost in the pages of some book, made shift to be where other people were, the larger the number the better he was pleased. His talk was informing, to be sure; but it was witty too and full of humor. He nearly always had a funny story to tell. Nobody could resist his funny stories, and he was fond of jokes as he was of reading.

By his sixteenth year he was six feet high and bony and raw, dark skinned.

As a teenager, he did not show any interested in hard labor. As a result of his distaste toward hard labor, he was labeled as a lazy and indolent lad. However, he soon broke this image and proved to be a responsible teen. He became a skillful axe man in his work involving rail fences.

He was also known for his brawn and audacity after he participated in many a competitive wrestling match. His long legs and arms gave him great advantage over his opponents. His reputation as a strong and talented wrestler contributed to his early success as a politician.

He would walk along the narrow forest trails, a faraway look in his eyes. No matter how much he learned, he wanted to learn more. He chuckled when he read something that amused him. He would be laughing one minute; the next minute he would look solemn and sad.

They laughed at him because he was so tall and awkward. They thought it was funny that his trousers were always too short. His shirt was in rags. His black hair was tousled. But they also laughed at his jokes, and they liked him.

He lifted his battered straw hat, and started down the path toward the field. He walked with dignity.

The fact that he could not carry a tune didn't seem to bother him.

He continued to write poetry as well as prose compositions long after his school days were over. He looked very dignified in a new suit and high pug hat.

When he was twenty-two years old, he decided to set out on his own. He relocated to the village of New Salem, Illinois. He was hired by a local businessman to transport goods by flatboat from New Salem to New Orleans through the Sangamon, Illinois, and Mississippi Rivers. Being brought up in slavery-free territories, he was shocked to witness the magnitude of slavery prevailing in New Orleans. At age twenty-three, he, along with a partner, bought a general store in New Salem on credit.

He didn't have much money. But when he became a lawyer, he wanted to look his best. He bought a long black coat and a tall black hat. For a long time he was poor, but little by little he paid off his debts. He knew that hard days lay ahead. Even then he had wanted to be President.

He spent Election Day in the telegraph office. Report after report came in from different parts of the country. He was gaining. He was winning.

His thoughts went back to his boyhood. He thought of all the people who had encouraged and helped him. He thought of his mother who, more than any one person, had given him a chance to get ahead.

- seventeen -

His life was one intense, unceasing, desperate struggle upwards with seemingly little attention to what the climb was all about.

When he was born, on December 29, 1808 in a little two-and-half story log cabin, his native Raleigh was still a raw settlement. In later years the story of his birth in a small building in the back of Casso's Inn became traditional. The story goes that his father and his mother worked at the hotel.

When one rises to distinction the world demands to know what were his ancestral relations, what his early environments, and what traits of character were prominent in youth. His ancestry can hardly be traced beyond his own father's family, and of these only enough is known to assure us that while they were poor, they were honorable and upright people.

His father was landless and illiterate; he made a living by engaging in various odd jobs, including milling, city constable, sexton, and porter to the State Bank. His mother was a seamstress and a laundress.

When he was only three years old, his father died after heroically saving three men from drowning.

Thus, his early environment was not promising. As a poor white boy in a small Southern town, he could not help but realize his lowly position. His family's lowly position undoubtedly made a deep impression on him. He could hardly miss feeling the striking contrast between himself and the elite. Unlike children of the rich, he never had a day's schooling in his life; his mother was too poor to afford it, and there were no public schools in Raleigh.

All schools charged tuition back then, and his family had little money. The admiral system of common or free schools, which are now enjoyed by the poor children of the whole country, is a blessing which at that time had not been experienced by North Carolina, and consequently he was never enabled to receive an hour's instruction in a schoolroom.

He never went to school one day in his life.

He was a swarthy complexioned, black-haired boy with deep, dark eyes. Described as a "wild and harum scarum" youngster, he was a member of a gang formed by his cousins.

When he and his cousins once ran across the path between the house of John Devereaux and that of his son, Devereaux sent his coachmen to whip the boys back to their shanty—they were running naked, according to Devereaux's granddaughter. (In another version of the story, he was given a whipping for trying to steal some fruit from one of Devereaux's daughters.)

Yet, poor though he was, he must have also realized that he was not at the very bottom of the social scale. After all, he was white, a fact that gave him a standing immeasurably higher than that of Raleigh's numerous blacks. Although he freely played with mulatto children, he certainly could not escape the ingrained racism so prevalent in Southern society.

He would never get over his childhood deprivation and the experience of being looked down upon by his so-called social betters.

But he was no ordinary boy. Though deprived of schooling and books, he had a zest for learning. On discovering that at Selby's tailor shop, where his brother was apprenticed, public-spirited citizens came to read to the tailors, he often came to listen. Then, when he himself was apprenticed to Selby, he became known to his fellow workers for his interest in obtaining an education.

He was taught the alphabet by fellow-workmen, borrowed

books and learned to read. Literacy came slowly for him (not until his late thirties was writing comparatively easy for him). For twelve hours a day, he and the other apprentices practiced the art of sewing. He was good at it.

He and his brother fled their apprenticeships after getting into a little trouble in Raleigh. A reward of $10 was posted for their return to their apprenticed tailor.

Applying himself steadily to his trade for his own and mother's support, he was left without any resource but his own exertions, and he thus began life struggling with the rough business world, but with a heart that stoutly battled poverty and misfortune. Through perseverance and patience, aided by a strong resolution to surmount all obstacles, success crowned his efforts; and to his great delight he found himself able to read the speeches to which he had only a short time before been an interested listener.

One who was a companion of his toil in Selby's tailor-shop has testified to the restless energy of the lad, which frequently brought him into trouble with his mistress, but adds that there were never any dishonorable traits of character manifested in his acts of mischief.

It is said that he fell passionately in love with a young lady of Laurens, and that, rather than marry before he had gotten a start in life, he ran away from the temptation, to which he was determined not to yield, and yet whose presence he dared not face.

After his experience as an apprentice, he determined never to work for any other man. He would have his own shop, and he would never have a partner in business. These resolutions he carried out, and they are an index to his whole life.

He was the very personification of independence. He did not wholly repose confidence in any man.

When he was sixteen, he moved to Laurens Court-House, South Carolina, where he worked as a journeyman tailor. Two years later, with his mother and stepfather, he set out in a two-wheeled cart, drawn by a blind pony, for Greenville, Tennessee. Here he married Eliza McCardle, a woman of refinement who read to him while he was at work and taught him to write. (He did not know how to write his own name on the marriage certificate.)

In the evenings, after he was done sewing, his wife taught him how to write and do simple math. He practiced his signature in the margins of his account books, but his spelling and writing skills never became polished.

- eighteen -

He was a child of the great Valley of Democracy.

Inside a little two-room cabin that stood by the great Ohio River, he was born on April 27, 1822. A picture of the house in which he was born shows it to have been a small frame dwelling of primitive character.

He was the oldest child in his family.

His mother possessed the traits of a strong willed but silent farm woman. Neighbors knew his father as a hard-working tanner who cured leather from hides of animals. His father was a talkative man who enjoyed arguing about politics.

His mother disbelieved in praise. Her detachment as a mother is hard to explain, especially since her attitude became stronger as he grew older.

When he was a boy, he was a small, skinny child, serious and sensitive. He was not good at sports and was only an average student.

He began attending Georgetown's subscription school when he was five. As he grew older, he showed a special skill at solving arithmetic problems in his head.

He showed a love for horses at an early age. He often played in the straw among the horses in his father's stables. By the age of five he could stand upon a trotting horse's back, balancing himself with the rains.
reins

At eight he could handle a wagon and team of horses. He even swung on horses' tales without any fear of being hurt by them.

In truth, he was quite a bashful young man. The town saw him as bashful, inferring that, because he did not talk much, he wasn't particularly bright.

But his knowledge of horses, of timber, and of land was better than his knowledge of men. He had no precocious "smartness," as the Yankees name the quality which enables one person to outwit another. His credulity was simple and unsuspecting, at least in some directions. This is illustrated by a story which he has told himself, one which he was never allowed to forget: "There was a Mr. Ralston, who owned a colt which I very much wanted. My father had offered twenty dollars for it, but Ralston wanted twenty-five. I was so anxious to have the colt that... my father yielded, but said twenty dollars was all the horse was worth, and told me to offer that price. If it was not accepted, I was to offer twenty-two and a half, and if that would not get him, to give the twenty-five. I at once mounted a horse and went for the colt. When I got to Mr. Ralston's house, I said to him: 'Papa says I may offer you twenty dollars for the colt, but, if you won't take that, I am to offer twenty-two and a half, and if you won't take that, to give you twenty-five.'" This naïve bargaining was done when he was eight years old.

He seemed unable to please his father and his mother showed an indifference to him that was remarked on even at the beginning of his life.

He suffered from migraine headaches.

He was drawn to experiences and work that challenged his practical ingenuity, such as contriving a means of moving heavy rocks or logs needed for his father's business. He evinced an early practical handiness—skill for doing, usually alone, practical things that needed to be done, taking particular pleasure in persevering until they were completed.

At home, his parents never felt a need to punish him. Classmates later recalled that he also behaved well in school.

He was a lad of self-reliance, fertile in resources, and of good judgment within certain limitations.

Being the eldest of an increasing family, it naturally happened that he was required to perform a share of work for its support, and to bear responsibilities. In his early youth his employment was in the farm work, and this he always preferred.

He hated working in his father's tannery. The bloody animal skins and smelly vats of curing chemicals made him sick to his stomach. But he found other ways to help his family. His mastery with horses sometimes earned him money when neighbors brought him untamed horses to break and train.

He was fond of all animals, and especially delighted in horses, early demonstrating a surprising power in managing them. He was locally noted for his success in breaking colts, and as a trainer of horses to be pacers, those having this gait being esteemed more desirable for riding, at a time when a large part of all traveling was done on horseback.

By fourteen he had established a livery service, owned and operated alone.

He learned his school tasks without great effort. His parents were alive to the advantages of education, and required him to attend all the subscription schools kept in the town. There were no free schools there during his youth.

He seems to have had good native powers of perception, reasoning, and memory. What he learned he kept, but he was never an ardent scholar. He had no enthusiasm for knowledge, nor, indeed, so far as appears, for anything else except horses.

He exhibited nothing of the young Napoleon's distemper of gnawing pride. He was just an ordinary American boy, with rather less boyishness and rather more sobriety than most, disposed to listen to the talk of his elders instead of that of persons of his own age, and fond of visiting strange places and riding and driving about the country.

He reluctantly agreed to attend West Point at his father's insistence.

He was only seventeen when he entered West Point. Although he was strong, he was small, still only 5 feet 1 inch tall and weighed only 117 pounds. On the way to West Point, he wished there might be a railroad or steamship accident. He wanted to be slightly injured—not badly, just enough to make him unable to attend.

Drum rolls shook him awake each dawn. He marched, drilled, and stood at attention for roll calls and inspection. He did love the countryside around West Point, perched on high cliffs overlooking the Hudson River.

Unlike many of his classmates, he was not interested in an army career. If he could graduate, he hoped he could gain an appointment as a junior math teacher at the academy for a few years, then find a teaching position in a college.

In his third term at West Point, he was promoted to sergeant, but he received so many demerits that he spent his fourth term there as a private. In the fall of 1843, he graduated 21st out of 39 students.

It was as a horseman that he made his greatest impression at West Point. He continued to excel at horsemanship. At graduation exercises, he set a high jump record that stood for twenty-five years.

Before reporting to his first post, he returned to Ohio for a three-month leave. While he was there, his new uniform was delivered. He put it on and rode into Cincinnati, expecting that he would receive much admiration. Instead, a young boy, barefoot and dirty, laughed at him. Even worse, when he returned home, he found a stable attendant dressed up in an imitation uniform parading about, getting big laughs. He felt humiliated. From then on he had a great dislike for fancy military uniforms.

- nineteen -

He was a posthumous child reared
among women, born October 4, 1822
in Delaware, Ohio.

He was a sickly child whose survival was at first doubtful. It was
his sister Fanny who was his protector and nurse, leading him
about the garden and on short visits to neighbors. He was able
to reciprocate when she in turn fell ill, giving her little rides upon
a sled during her recovery.

His father, a New Englander born in West Brattleboro, Vermont,
was descended from a long line of Presbyterians who had come
from Scotland in 1625 to settle in Connecticut.

His mother was a descendant of an old New England family,
whose paternal ancestor had arrived in America from England
in 1634.

As his health improved, his mother began to rejoice in her child.
The relief that accompanied his improved health was shattered
when his brother Lorenzo drowned while ice-skating.

His mother would always fear for his life and watched him
anxiously.

He was a handsome, large-hearted boy, a blue-eyed, auburn-
haired boy who enjoyed playing with his sister's dolls before he
was given toy soldiers.

He was seven years old before his mother allowed him to play
with other children and nine before she permitted him to
participate in strenuous sports.

He and his sister Fanny shared a tendency to be irreverent in their puns and jokes, which their pious mother tolerated but did not encourage.

His teacher wrote in a letter to his mother: He has applied himself industriously to his studies and he has maintained a constant and correct deportment. I think he will avail himself of the advantage of an education and fully meet the just anticipation of his friends. He is well informed, has good sense, and is respected and esteemed by his companions. He is strictly economical and regular in his habits and has established a very favorable character among us.

He was not fazed by his studies; on composition day, he wrote an essay about Liberty, and on speaking day, he delivered a eulogy on Lord Chatham, both well done.

He studied Latin and Greek. Although at first it was hard to keep up with the class, he quickly succeeded.

He took long walks in the hills. He studied French. He stuffed his pockets with buckeye nuts, home-whittled tops, knives, and rocks.

The slender little boy with the reddish hair dawdled over his breakfast porridge. For him this was strange. Usually, since the passing of the frailty that had marked his infancy, he was quick and cheerful at meals.

His trusting blue eyes were lively.

His house, of two stories with a brick front, really was a pleasant place. The trouble was, all the menfolk in his house were gone. Only females were left there with him—his mother, his sister, and his mother's spinster cousin, Arcena Smith.

He knew—no boy could have known it more clearly—that he was loved in his house. Sometimes his mother's hug of him was too hard and lingering, as if she were reaching for someone else.

His mother was overfond of talking to him, in serious tones of God and heaven and salvation. He liked better the stories about knights and giants and cats in boots in his books.

As a boy, he struggled with a severe irrational fear: lyssophobia, the fear of going insane.

He made no distinction of sex in his feelings about people in the world. But this neuter stage in his growth was going. He knew that he was a man-child.

He was a friendly person who liked people in general—and always would be so. There was something appealing and magnetic about his personality already that attracted people of all kinds, causing women to wish to mother him and even rough men to pat his head or take his hand.

Nor was this wholly because he was a fatherless boy who made up for being fatherless by being especially friendly toward adults. His marked friendliness was deep in his nature.

He eagerly took in the talk of men. He repeated as well as he could manly stories and mimicked masculine mannerisms.

When his mother read to him, the book was usually *Pilgrim's Progress*.

He was naturally high-spirited, and his mother often had to correct his manners and tell him to quiet down.

He and Fanny began to attend the new public school in Delaware. He recalled, the school was free to all and was crowded with scholars of all ages, from little folks of our own size up to young men grown.

Despite his years of isolation from other children, he was outgoing and friendly. He loved his life, his hometown, and his country.

When he was eleven, he travelled to New England, where many of his relatives still lived. He enjoyed all the different modes of transportation used on the trip, from old-fashioned stagecoach to brand-new railroad, from river steamboat to canal boat on the Erie Canal.

He excelled in logic, mental and moral philosophy, and mathematics, and also made his mark as a debater in the literary societies.

In October 1837, he said goodbye to his mother and headed east to Isaac Webb's Preparatory School, in Middletown, Connecticut. His childhood was over. But in many ways, his fun was just beginning.

He did well at the Webb School and earned the headmaster's praise. Despite the heavy workload, he found time for play. He went ice-skating and played ball. He and his friends took long hikes on Saturday afternoons.

His uncle proposed that he attend the Webb School for one more year, in preparation of Yale. He, however, believed he was already sufficiently prepared for college. His mother thought he had spent enough time in the East. She wanted him back in his home state and decided that he should attend Kenyon College in Gambier, Ohio. He agreed with his mother, and he left Connecticut, heading for home. Just after his sixteenth birthday, he set foot in Delaware, Ohio for the first time in a year.

In 1838 he entered Kenyon College at Gambier, Ohio. There, too, he established an excellent record. Enjoying his college career, he made several lasting friendships, among them future Supreme Court Justice Stanley Matthews.

It was at Kenyon that he started his diary, an invaluable source for his career, which he continued to keep to the end of his life.

As valedictorian, he addressed the school president, whom he praised for his closeness to the students, the faculty, and his fellow students. Soon afterward he began to study law in the office of Thomas Sparrow, and then attended a course of law lectures at Harvard University.

For years his relationship with this lovely sister Fanny was overly close, for a long time threatening the true fulfillment and happiness of his marriage.

- twenty -

He was born on November 19, 1831 in a log cabin in Orange Township, Ohio.

As his mother fondly recalled, he was "the largest Babe I ever had; he looked like a red Irishman." His father died two years later, and he was raised in poverty in a household led by a strong-willed mother.

The humble log cabin he was born in was about twenty feet one way by thirty the other, and it had three small windows, a dirt floor, and the spaces between the logs of which it was built were filled in with clay.

He lived in a day when all literature, including biography, was expected to perform a moral function; when the loves of great men, as the poet said, were designed to teach us that we could make our lives sublime.

His father died in debt, so his mother sold off fifty acres to pay their creditors, leaving thirty, which, with her own industry and that of her oldest son, served to maintain her little family.

As a toddler he was bright and restless. He was a very good-natured child. He walked when he was nine months old. When he was ten months old he would climb the fence, go up the ladder a dozen times a day. He was never still a minute at a time. Always uneasy, very quick to learn.

Within the song-filled circle of his family, he passed a happy childhood. His mother had the gift of banishing care from her hearth.

He displayed a certain precocity. When he was only three, his sister carried him through the woods to the little red district

78

school house, and soon he was delighting his proud family by reading from the Bible.

His family were neither squatters nor paupers, but even with the help of neighbors, their household lived near the raw edge of poverty.

There was no house within a mile of his, and the village a mile and a half away contained only a school-house, a grist-mill, and a little log store and dwelling.

He was four years old before he had his first pair of shoes.

Often he could be seen perched on the top of a tree, with a pail, picking cherries for his mother to preserve, or gathering apples for her to dry. Out-door life to the boy, who had already toddled through infancy and was now a rousing youngster of eight, presented many an attraction that some children never seem to perceive.

He went to school and obtained such knowledge of the mysteries of grammar, arithmetic, and geography as could be obtained in the common schools of that day.

He learned that he was poor and that he was an orphan.

The school-house was so far away that his mother, who appreciated the importance of education for her children, offered her neighbors a site for a new school-house on her own land, and one was built. Here winter after winter came teachers, some of limited qualifications, to instruct the children of the neighborhood, and here he enlarged his stock of book-learning by slow degrees.

Poor and fatherless, he was mocked by his fellow boys, and remained sensitive to slights throughout his life. These boyhood wounds left a lasting scar on his personality.

He escaped through reading, devouring all the books he could find. From his earliest appreciable days, he had been fond of books. What he could obtain in the way of literature he devoured, not merely read, but re-read and re-read.

As a boy he was always a busy spectator and assistant at the various harvest ceremonies; cider making, apple gathering for butter, corn husking and the like. And when the hay was turned to dry in the sun, he raked it into windrows for the pitchers.

He had an active temperament, and would have been happiest when busy, even if he had not known that his mother needed the fruits of his labor. He was a stout boy, with the broad shoulders and sturdy frame of his former ancestors, and he was sure he could give satisfaction.

His older brother was quiet, unambitious, and aspired to nothing more than the honest, regular round of a farmer's life, while he, the younger, was enterprising, ambitious and pushing in his temperament. It is more than doubtful if he ever intended to be a farmer, and, probably, from his earliest years his brain was tenanted with visions of greatness.

He had a carpenter's bench, and on this he worked early and late, though his labor brought him but small financial return. He had now become so expert in the use of tools that he could, while yet a mere boy, make or build almost anything, and his talent as a carpenter was in constant demand. Hardly a building or enterprise of any kind in the section of Ohio where he lived but bore some marks of his skill.

Inclined to be a stubborn, willful boy, he required careful handling, his mother believed. One year, for example, tiring of the weekly three-mile tramp through the woods to attend church, he refused to go. His mother received this rebellion with unexpected calm, and agreed that he could stay home on Sunday, stipulating only that he was not to leave the house. A year of this weekly house arrest was too much for his restless nature, and when his term was over he docilely returned to church.

As he grew into adolescence, he began to develop traits that disturbed his mother. An overgrown, uncombed, unwashed boy, he was moody and belligerent by turns. Frequently he picked fights with the boys who crossed him. More often, however, he withdrew into himself, framing mighty plans and transaction of which he was always the hero.

At Geauga Academy, he learned academic subjects he had not previously had time for. He shone as a student, and was especially interested in languages and elocution. He began to appreciate the power a speaker had over an audience, writing that the speaker's platform "creates some excitement; I love agitation and investigation and glory in defending unpopular truth against popular error."

At fifteen, he was a strong, sturdy boy, with a mass of auburn hair. He had a bright, intelligent face, and an earnest look that attracted general attention.

His dreams were fed by books. Next to hunting, reading was his greatest passion. Books were rare, but those he had were devoured over and over until they could be reeled off from memory. He liked history, especially those stirring stories of the American Revolution that reminded him of the ballads his mother loved to sing. Fiction, however, was his chief delight, especially stories of faraway places.

The thought of running away to sea took hold of him with an obsessive grasp. His drab landlocked existence seemed intolerable.

He left home at age sixteen. A strong, sturdy boy, with a mass of auburn hair, partly covered by a loose-fitting hat, he had a bright, intelligent face, and an earnest look that attracted general attention. In his rustic garb he was not well enough dressed to act as clerk in a Cleveland store.

Then rejected by the only ship in port in Cleveland, he found work on a canal boat. No one complained that he was not well enough attired for a canal-boy. He was responsible for the mules that pulled the boat.

On the canal, he worked six hours on and six hours off. He did not have to wait long after his engagement before he was put on duty. With boyish pride he mounted one of the mules and led the other. A line connected his mules with the boat, which was drawn slowly and steadily through the water. He felt the responsibility of his situation.

After six weeks, his canal career came to an abrupt end. He fell sick with the "ague." Too weak to work, he stumbled back to home and mother, and fell into his old bed.

In his late teens, he underwent a religious awakening, and attended many camp meetings, at one of which he was born again. The next day, March 4, 1850, he was baptized by being submerged in the icy waters of the Chagrin River.

He attended the Western Reserve Eclectic Institute (later named Hiram College) in Hiram, Ohio. While there, he was most interested in the study of Greek and Latin, but was inclined to learn about and discuss any new thing he encountered. Securing a position on entry as janitor, he was hired to teach while still a student.

He then enrolled at Williams College in Williamstown, Massachusetts, as a third-year student, given credit for two years' study at the Institute after passing a cursory examination.

After his first term, he was hired to teach penmanship to the students of nearby Pownal, Vermont—a post whose previous incumbent was Chester A. Arthur.

He graduated from Williams in August 1856 as salutatorian, giving an address at the commencement.

- twenty-one -

He was born October 5, 1829, in Fairfield, Vermont.

On his father's side he was Scotch-Irish. He was the oldest of a family of two sons and five daughters.

His mother met his father while he was teaching at a school in Dunham, just over the border. His mother was of Canadian birth and has been described by an acquaintance as a large, lively, good-natured woman who was much esteemed by her acquaintances.

His father was a Free Will Baptist minister who became an outspoken abolitionist, which often made him unpopular with members of his congregation and contributed to the family's frequent moves. His family's frequent moves later spawned accusations that he was not a native-born citizen of the United States.

His father had a stable income and was able to shield the family from the economic tumult of the time.

In 1832, his family finally settled in the Schenectady, New York, area.

A teacher would recall: His eyes were dark and brilliant, and his physical system finely formed. He was frank and open in his manners, and genial in his disposition.

He loved to fish.

By the time he was ten years old, he had lived in no less than five homes.

Unlike his father, who often angered peopled, he had an agreeable, friendly personality. Like his father, he was an abolitionist.

A companion of his in Union Village remembered that he once watched the village boys build a mud dam after a rain shower, and, after a while, began telling the boys how to build the dam better. They followed his instructions without question, even though he took care not to get any of the dirt and mud on his hands.

He first attended school at the academy in Union Village. Shortly after the family moved to Schenectady he was placed for the winter in the Lyceum to prepare for entrance at Union College.

An able and intelligent student, he took time away from the heavily classical curriculum to co-edit *The Lyceum Review*, a school newspaper that featured short sermons, poetry, and campus news.

He received his first instruction from his father. He entered Union College as a sophomore at the age of fifteen. As a student, he engaged in undergraduate high-jinx and enjoyed playing school pranks.

At school, he joined other young Whigs in support of Henry Clay, even participating in a brawl against students who supported James K. Polk. He showed more interest in extracurricular activities and politics than his studies.

He lived on campus with the other students and could not leave without permission. His letters to friends revealed a quiet sense of humor and fondness for a good story.

He studied what any undergraduate studied in those years—the Greek and Roman classics in their original, which would have been taught mostly by rote. And as with any undergraduate, his passion for Homer, Livy, and Cicero was lukewarm at best. According to the few accounts we have, he was an average student in most ways, average in grades and average in his occasional transgressions.

He seemed to prefer parties and socializing with classmates to schoolwork. College authorities fined him for skipping chapel. He also got caught throwing the school bell in the Erie Canal and jumping on and off slow moving trains.

But he also kept up with his classes. Like other students, he began the school day with breakfast at 6:30 a.m., and he finished with a 7:00 p.m. study session. To help with college expenses, he taught children in nearby schools during winter vacation.

He became president of the college's debate society.

In his senior year he wore a green coat occasionally to show his sympathy for the Fennian movement. He managed to be elected to Phi Beta Kappa, along with the top third of the seventy-nine-member graduating class.

At graduation he gave a speech titled "The Destiny of Genius."

After leaving college, he taught at a country school during two years in Vermont, and then, having managed by rigid economy to save about $500, he started for New York, and entered the law office of ex-Judge E. D. Culver as a student.

He was later admitted to the bar and practiced law in New York City.

He got his license to practice law in May 1854, and he was hired to take the case of Elizabeth Jennings, an African American teacher who was forcibly removed from a whites-only streetcar on the Third Avenue Line in New York City. At the trial, he showed the judge a new section of the New York laws that related to common carriers—vehicles used by the public. After hearing his argument, the judge told the jury that the Third Avenue Railroad Company was responsible for the actions of its streetcar conductors, and the judge further ruled that "colored persons, if sober, well-behaved, and free from disease" could not be forced off streetcars and other types of public transportation.

- twenty-two -

On March 18ᵗʰ, 1837, he was born. There was nothing whatever remarkable about him as a baby, for he was even considered slight and small at first, although vigorously healthy. It must be said, however, that he came into the world surrounded by every necessary care and comfort, and with every advantage except wealth.

Even in the cradle, it is said that he exhibited signs of uncommon persistency and strength of will.

He was the fifth of nine children.

His mother was originally from Baltimore, the daughter of a bookseller.

His father was a Presbyterian minister.

His first three years were passed at the Caldwell (New Jersey) parsonage, and then that home was exchanged for another every way as quiet and as rural, a few miles from what would become the city of Syracuse, New York.

His father believed it was never too early to commence a child's education; his children learned while still toddlers the Puritanical obedience in which the family was steeped.

When he was four years old, his father was called as pastor to yet another church.

As a boy he received the usual strict training.

Often as a boy he was compelled to get out of his warm bed at night to hang up a hat or other garment which he had left on the floor. He was also obliged to comply with the biblical commandments, commit to memory the Westminster Catechism, and comport himself in a manner consonant with Puritan conviction.

Neighbors described him as full of fun and prone to play pranks.

His upbringing taught him that there is a right which is eternally right, and wrong which must remain forever wrong. Such training accounted for his tendency to view all matters, great and small, in absolute terms—just or unjust, right or wrong, black or white—as well as for the duality of his nature. This duality caused contemporaries to see in him two antipathetic personalities.

His earliest recorded ambition was kindled by the idea of someday becoming a student of the village academy, but he had to endure, first, a preparatory course of two years in a very red, wooden, unbeautiful district schoolhouse. He entered this, for the first time, when he was eight years old, and the course of study he was then pursuing included every right good place for digging bait, or for enticing fish with it afterward, which a small boy could obtain knowledge of and hope to profit by.

He was young, barely eleven; he was sturdy rather than large for his age, and he was brimming with exultation over the important victory he had won in getting into the academy.

Nuts and berries and many other important elements of natural history were also receiving his thorough and conscientious attention. Day after day, during those two district school years, he saw the favored students of the academy go and come to and from the dignified belfry-crowned structure so near to his own home, but seemingly so far from him. Many of those students seemed to be only a few inches taller than himself. They were getting wiser and wiser all the while, he knew, and they had all sorts of fun, to which he was as yet an outsider. He begged his father again and again for promotion from the district school to the academy, but those few inches were in the way, and so were a vague number of months of time.

Once the books were put away, he was as ready for fun as was any other youngster in town, and those of near his own age were even willed to acknowledge a kind of leadership that was not at all weakened by his superiority in the recitation room.

Despite his father's dedication to his missionary work, the income was insufficient for the large family. Financial conditions forced him to be removed from school into a two-year mercantile apprenticeship in Fayetteville. The experience was valuable and brief, and his living conditions quite austere. He returned home and to his schooling at the completion of the contract.

He was conscious that his people were patriots whose deeds were tied to the history of the country. He knew much about national heroes. When he was only nine years old, in writing a composition on the value of industriousness, he pointed out: "George Washington improved his time when he was a boy and he was not sorry when he was at the head of a large army fighting for his country...Jackson was a poor boy but he was placed in school and by improving his time he found himself President of the United States guiding and directing a powerful nation."

During his boyhood years, he grew into a hearty, fun-loving young man with a strong constitution and an equally strong sense of responsibility.

He showed himself to be a diligent, solid student and looked forward to attending nearby Hamilton College.

He was sixteen when his father died. It became necessary for him to set aside his college plans and work in support of his mother and the four siblings still at home.

Although his formal schooling had ended, nineteenth-century academic standards ensure that he was well educated. For example, though not an exceptional student, he had studied Latin, working on translating Virgil's Aeneid. The caliber of his adult writings and speeches would be creditable for a college graduate today.

He would wait until he was out on his own before viewing life in other than puritanical terms. A deist in the Jeffersonian sense, he believed in God, but not in all the man-crafted accretions to that belief.

He first worked as a bookkeeper and assistant teacher in the literary department at the New York Institute for the Blind in New York City, a position suggested to him by his older brother, who had come to Hamilton College and had taught at the institution himself.

His living quarters at the state-supported school were cold, the food was poor, and the children suffered from a lack of love and attention. He left after a year and never looked back fondly on his time at the institution.

He soon moved to Buffalo after visiting with an uncle who was a prosperous cattle breeder with a farm at Black Rock, just outside the city.

His uncle found him employment with the law firm Rogers, Bowen & Rogers, where he performed routine tasks like copying documents while studying in the firm's law library and learning from its attorneys in preparation for the bar examination. His diligence and intelligence impressed his employers. Soon he earned his license to practice law.

He enjoyed the social life of Buffalo's beer halls. Women seemed not to figure in his social life.

- twenty-three -

He was born on August 20, 1833,
at North Bend, Ohio, on the Ohio River
west of Cincinnati, in the home of his
illustrious grandfather.

He was born into a family that was very active in serving its country. His great-grandfather was a signer of the Declaration of Independence. His grandfather was the ninth president of the United States. His father served as a U.S. congressman.

His mother was a devout and active Presbyterian and raised her children in that faith.

His father earned just enough money to hold onto his land and educate his children. His family grew much of its own food. His mother and sisters made most of the family's clothing.

Growing up on the Point, which is what his father's farm was called, he enjoyed his life of farm chores, attending a log cabin school, and especially fishing in the Ohio River and hunting along its banks. From the family's front porch he could watch flatboats and steamships heading down the river as settlers continued to push the frontier west.

In the summer of 1840, when he turned seven years old, his family and friends in North Bend, Ohio were in a dither of excitement. The Whig party had nominated his grandfather to run for president. As a favorite grandson, he must have been excited and pleased by the campaign for his grandfather, who was elected to the presidency that fall.

Despite his father's financial troubles, he enjoyed a happy childhood.

He liked to read too, and for this appetite his grandfather's well-stocked library was a godsend. At his mother's urging, he read Bunyan's *Pilgrim's Progress*.

He never got to visit his grandfather in the White House. Only weeks after his grandfather became president, he fell ill with pneumonia and died.

He had the usual amount of stone bruises and stubbed toes and average number of nails in his foot that fell to the portion of farmers' boys.

Though the supply of teachers was limited, his parents always employed a tutor or a nurse who guaranteed that the ABCs would not be neglected.

There is little doubt that his family background helped to mold him. He was ever conscious of the fact that he should live up to the great traditions of his family.

He was a farmer's boy, lived in a little farmhouse, had to hustle out of bed between 4 and 5 o'clock in the morning the year round to feed stock, get ready to drop corn or potatoes, or rake hay by the time the sun was up. He knew how to feed the pigs, how to teach a calf how to drink milk out of a bucket, could harness a horse in the dark, and do all the things farmer's boys new how to do.

He used to go to the mill on a sack of wheat or corn and balance it over the horse's back by getting on one end of it, holding on to the horse's mane while he was going uphill, and feeling anxious about the results.

Before he would be allowed to set out on an expedition into the woods for squirrels or out on the river for fish or ducks, his father insisted that he always have the company of an elder. He showed a spar of genius in complying with the paternal injunction. For very frequently he assisted the Negro who served the household in the capacity of cook; he carried wood and water for the Negro, and helped him wash the dishes that he might better secure his company in a bout at fishing or hunting.

When he was fourteen, he and his brother were sent to a boarding school in Cincinnati.

He liked schoolboy sports and used to half-walk and half-run to school in order to get there in time to play bullpen for half an hour before books.

He had far more than intellectual brilliance—he had character.

He spoke in a soft, melodious voice, but behind the voice, as behind the face, was an element of strength.

He grew up, at first a slender, wiry stripling, and bit by bit became a chubby, square-shouldered boy, so blond as to be almost white-haired.

Though not the rollicking type, he cultivated more than a few friends. He was not selfish.

He had his likes and his dislikes, was somewhat careless of his external appearance, and yet left the overall impression with his fellow students as an unpretentious but courageous student... respectable in language and science...and excellent in political science and history...who talked easily and fluently and never seemed to regard life as a joke nor opportunities for advancement as subject for sport.

He showed great promise as a student, and his father hoped to send him to an eastern college such as Yale. But in the summer of 1850, his mother died and his father decided that he should study closer to home. He was sent to Miami University, a publicly supported college in Oxford, Ohio.

While he was acclimating himself to Oxford and a new group of friends, he was much perturbed that his family failed to write him. He was soon seriously distracted from his studies by the lack of news from home. Finally, his sister wrote: "Pa has not written because he wants to wait until he can send you money."

He was remembered as spending many profitable hours in the library. When he spoke, he impressed his fellow debaters as level headed and thoughtful and one who usually made a thorough preparation.

As an acknowledgement of his skill in public speaking and as a personal tribute from his colleagues, he was elected the presidency of the Union Literary Society.

Everything pointed to his career as a gentleman of the cloth: the exceptionally deep religious character of his parents who recognized in practice the supremacy of things of the spirit; the very campus of Miami, where professors were purportedly living models of sanctity; the effect of frequent religious revivals on his thinking; and his own whole-hearted acceptance of Presbyterianism and his solemn promise to enter the ministry.

After he graduated from Miami University, he considered entering the Presbyterian ministry, but decided instead to study law. He went to Cincinnati to serve as an unpaid apprentice in a law firm, studying under one of the attorneys there. He drove himself to study long hours.

With a warmth and a vigor that possibly give a clue to his ultimate choice, he pondered the merits of the legal profession.

He willingly admitted that "the legal profession has not yet arrived at that dignity and moral excellence to which it could be brought…" Yet in his opinion the blame must be borne by the public whose estimate of this profession has been so low "that many who would have given a higher moral tone to it, have been prevented from entering upon it by the notion…that no Christian could consistently do so."

He married early and was particularly fortunate in having a wife who fulfilled all the requirements of an ideal helpmate.

- twenty-four -

ditto
chapter twenty-two
pages 98-102

"...There is little doubt that his family background helped to mold him. He was ever conscious of the fact that he should live up to the great traditions of his family...."

- twenty-five -

The house where he was born on January 29, 1843 was a small frame cottage, standing on a corner of the main street in the village of Niles, Ohio.

Of nine children in his family, he was seventh.

His ancestors came from the Scottish Highlands, where they were famous for their independence. Ancestors on both sides of his family were iron workers and tinkers.

His father was often absent from the family on business.

He got his share of attention, but his mother did not dote on him.

His mother said: "I don't believe I did raise the boy to be President. I tried to bring up the boy to be a good man, and this is the best that any mother can do. The first thing I knew, my son turned around and began to raise me to be the mother of a President."

Though his family lacked intellectual pretensions, they encouraged study.

He early exhibited two traits that he carried through manhood—a reluctance to talk, and acute powers of observation.

School intrigued him. It challenged him, and he enjoyed the arduous tasks of copying and memorizing for recitation. He seldom fell behind in his work and was adept at accomplishing the tasks assigned him.

From the first he had an uncanny ability to judge people in conversation, and to see solutions to problems through reflection and insight. His real education never came from books, however much he liked study, but from observation. Personal charm, willingness to work, and common sense sharpened his insight into the people and events around him.

Although he constantly associated with the boys of the village, who were not better than other lads, and no doubt occasionally used 'bad words," it was noticed by them that he never indulged in such language. They learned, too, that even when quite young he preferred to study his lessons before playing rather than after, declaring that he could have more fun when the work was out of the way. Gradually he came to be recognized as a natural commander. The boys looked up to him and accepted his word as law.

It had been noticed by his mates in the little one-story schoolhouse that when the time came for 'speaking pieces,' he stood up 'straight as a stick' and spoke without apparent effort—much to the chagrin of the other boys and girls to whom this part of their schooling was a dreaded ordeal.

In the spring and autumn he went fishing in Little Beaver Creek, sometimes camping out for a week at a time.

In 1852 his family moved from Niles, Ohio to Poland, Ohio so the children could attend an academy that was founded by New Englanders. His family home in Poland was a white frame dwelling with green blinds, and had a rising sun painted over the gable window.
His mother and her sisters had charge of the Methodist church in Niles, and swept, scrubbed, painted, and tended it with the same efficient thoroughness they applied to their own hearths and homes.

A former schoolmate recalls that he was a stout, pleasant-faced boy, who enjoyed playing with the other lads, and took a lively interest in their sports.

He always looked a trifle cleaner and neater than the other boys—no doubt his mother could explain why—and he always acted like a gentleman. Yet he was never a prig and did not think himself as better than others. On the contrary, he was well liked by his playmates. It was commonly remarked that he was 'good at anything he goes at.' He never had any quarrels.

Practically, his parents were very strong abolitionists, and he early imbibed very radical views regarding the enslavement of the colored race. When he was young he often visited the local tannery, usually full of Democrats, and argued about the slavery question. His eloquence and knowledge were put to good use, but he converted no one.

As a boy he played a game called "Old Sow," in which a block of wood was maneuvered into a hole with a stick, a childish version of golf.

He fished occasionally, swam with friends, and once almost drowned.

He was a great hand for marbles and he was very fond of his bows and arrows. The thing he loved best of all was a kite.

When summer came he always had a stone bruise. His shoes came off before the snow had left the ground.

He loved to go barefoot. In going barefoot, when he stubbed a toe or bruised a foot, he was proud as a king in showing the injury to the other boys.

His main chore was driving the milk cows into the lot morning and evening.

He studied after school and devoted much time to preparing materials for debates. Though he had bouts with sickness, he was usually healthy and anxious to join in games with playmates.

He had an aptitude for the practical; toward theoretical things his attitude was indifferent. His mind was always essentially retentive rather than creative.

He never cared much for pets.

At fifteen, he felt strong enough in his faith to be baptized into the Niles Methodist Church at a camp meeting. It gave him optimism that God's plan was working in his life and in the world.

His efforts to discover God's design produced a devout piety. His sincere lifelong adherence to Methodism in part reflected a deep attachment to his mother, who longed to give one of her sons to the ministry.

The Christian acceptance of life's tribulations in "Nearer My God to Thee" made it his favorite hymn.

His health broke down completely at Allegheny College, Meadville, Pennsylvania, and he came home and taught school when seventeen years of age.

In 1861 he promptly enlisted in the 23rd Ohio Volunteers and saw four years of service, beginning as a Private and ending as a Major. At Antietam, as a Private, he carried pails of hot coffee and food to the men on the firing line down by the creek, and was made Second Lieutenant for bravery. His courage at Winchester raised him to be Captain. He served gallantly also at Cedar Creek and became a Major.

Generals George Cook and Rutherford B. Hayes both knew him as a brave youth. The four years of outdoor army life, mainly in the mountains and highlands of Virginia, had given him perfect health.

After the war, he considered making the army a career but declined the commission after his father argued that prospects for advancement in the peacetime military would be poor.

He decided on the law.

He left Poland, Ohio to study law in Albany, New York, where he learned something of the ways of New York politicians.

He would train for the law as Abraham Lincoln had—by finding an attorney who would let him read law books in his office until he mastered the subjects and could pass the bar.

Encouraged by his sister, he entered Albany School of Law. His roommate recalled he "worked very hard, often reading until one or two in the morning." He ate ice cream for the first time at a reception after the dean's daughter explained the concept.

- twenty-six -

Born on October 27, 1858 in a four-story brownstone at 28 East 20th Street in Manhattan, he was the second of four children.

His family also included two sisters and a brother.

Inspecting her son the morning following his birth, his mother said, with Southern frankness, that he looked like a terrapin. He weighed eight and a half pounds, and was more than usually noisy.

His family was rich and powerful. Few Americans, surely, have been born into such a perfectly balanced home environment as he.

His mother was a socialite who had grown up in Georgia, where her family owned a plantation. His father and his grandfather were important businessmen in New York City.

Scattered references in family letters indicate a bright, hyperactive infant. Yet already the first of a succession of congenital ailments was beginning to weaken him. Asthma crowded his lungs, depriving him of sleep.

Even before he could read, he discovered a copy of *David Livingston's Missionary Travels and Researches in Southern Africa* in the family library and was fascinated by the illustrations of exotic birds and animals.

When he was a young boy, he was always small in size. His most serious illness was asthma.

Whether he was running a race or sitting still with a book, he never knew when he would suddenly find himself struggling for breath. He coughed, sneezed, wheezed, had raging fevers, and hardly ate. His asthma was so bad he had to sleep sitting up in bed or in a big chair.

His anxious parents tried many different remedies. Once they had him smoke a cigar, and another time they made him drink strong black coffee.

Until he got his glasses, he could only see things very close up. But that didn't stop him from studying photographs for hours of hippopotami with canoes on their backs and zebras racing across the African plains. He gobbled up books about the soldiers at Valley Forge and frontiersmen Davy Crockett and Daniel Boone.

For the first time, he could distinguish things more than a few feet in front of him and, marveling, declared: "I had no idea how beautiful the world was until I got those spectacles…"

A pale child with a shock of unruly fair hair, prominent teeth, and nearsighted blue eyes, he was almost a caricature of the pampered, protected child.

He also developed a form of nervous diarrhea, which he called "cholera morbus." He also suffered from a recurring dream of a werewolf waiting to spring upon him from the foot of his bed.

He won't live another year, predicted his Aunt Annie, shaking her head over his pale complexion and scrawny body.
When he was vomiting or had diarrhea, he said, I have a toothache in my stomach, it seemed that he would not live to see his fourth birthday.

Eager to learn, the young scientist snared all kinds of animals and preserved them for study. He was particularly attracted to the tales of Captain Mayne Reid with their simplified natural history and outdoor adventure.

He illustrated and wrote books about ants, spiders, ladybugs, fireflies, hawks, minnows, and crayfish. His fingers were always stained with ink. He collected animal and bird specimens and created a museum in his room. He smelled.

He noted every experience in his diary.

From his father, he inherited a sturdy Dutch character. From his mother, he acquired several refined French traits.

His liveliness, abnormal even for a small boy, was something of a trial to his languid mother.

When he was just seven, he watched the funeral procession for assassinated president Abraham Lincoln as it passed solemnly through the streets of New York. From the second-floor windows in his grandfather's house in New York City he watched the funeral parade—11,000 military men, 75,000 ordinary citizens, and the coffin pulled by a team of sixteen black-robed horses. President Lincoln was his hero.

Squinting through his glasses and grinning with his big teeth, the growing teenager continued his studies in natural history.
Soon he realized he possessed a photographic memory, enabling him to remember completely everything he read.

He did not attend public school. Like other rich children of the day, tutors taught him at home.

One recent biographer argues that some of his asthma attacks were largely self-induced in order to avoid attending the forbidding church services of the day.

When he reached ten, his father took him aside and said, "You have the mind but you have not the body. You must *make* your body."

Suddenly, he saw himself as this "little ape," a puny, gangly lad with pipestem arms and legs.

On the second floor porch of the family brownstone, his father installed athletic equipment for his son. Day after day the boy lifted barbells, swung chest weights, and exercised on parallel bars. He also took boxing lessons.

His skinny chest and muscles grew. But he was still sickly.

Nevertheless, he was chagrined to discover that his determined regimen of bodybuilding had not had much effect.

He had been a timid child in New York City, cut off from schoolboy society by illness, wealth, and private tutors. Inspired by his leonine father, he had labored with weights to build up his strength. Simultaneously, he had built up his courage "by sheer dint of practicing fearlessness."

Jerking his head back, he said through clenched teeth: "I'll make my body."

He exercised throughout the winter and spring of 1870-1871. Fiber by fiber his muscles tautened, while the skinny chest expanded by degrees perceptible only to himself.

He told a friend that his compulsive effort to build himself up was spurred not only by the desire to please his father, but by the shock of recognition after chancing upon Robert Browning's poem *The Flight of the Duchess*:

> ...The prettiest little ape
> That ever affronted human shape.
> ...All legs and length,
> With blood for bone, all speed, not strength.

He learned to move quickly and quietly to catch turtles, snakes, and lizards. He listened intently to the songs of thrushes, sparrows, and other birds, and soon he could identify many birds by their calls.

The day he saw a dead seal was the day he decided to become a zoologist.

He ran and hiked and played games. He even went swimming in some icy rapids--and said he enjoyed it.

At dinner one night, one of his mice poked its head from a Dutch cheese being passed around the table.

Another time, the family's cook was horrified to find a dead mouse in the icebox, placed here until needed for one of his experiments. He mourned after the mouse was thrown out, "Oh, the loss to science."

When he was thirteen, his father let have him a gun. The excited boy wanted to learn to hunt, but he soon discovered that his poor eyesight made it difficult for him to hit a target.

Over the next few years he grew into a gawky, tousle-haired teenager who reminded acquaintances of a stork, a resemblance accentuated by a habit of reading at his desk while standing on one leg with the other drawn up.

Tutored at home, he had not mixed with other youngsters and had been spared their taunts about his spindly appearance and his thick eyeglasses. On a trip to a camp at Moosehead Lake in Maine after a severe asthma attack when he was fourteen, two boys of about his own age made fun of him. The boys made life miserable for him. Deeply wounded by the experience, he persuaded his father to allow him to take boxing lessons. He began working out with John Lang, an ex-prizefighter.

His parents took the family on a twelve-month tour of Europe. Although he said he "cordially hated" that year, he also had fun. Indeed, his diary shows that they visited eight countries and stayed in sixty-six hotels.

A few years later, his family traveled to the Middle East. He was particularly fascinated with Egypt. While on a trip up the Nile River, he marveled at Alexandria, Cairo, Thebes, the Pyramids of Giza, and the various tombs and temples along the way

He had reached his full height of five feet eight inches tall. He remained thin, but he had grown strong, thanks to his exercise program

He never seemed to know what idleness was, said one of his tutors. His discipline took him through three years of college preparation in twenty-four months. At seventeen he passed Harvard's entrance exam and moved to Cambridge, Massachusetts, where he was a misfit, a slender, nervous young man with side-whiskers, eyeglasses, and bright red cheeks, and poorly equipped for social contacts. His room teemed with stuffed animals and birds; the smell of formaldehyde trailed him around the campus. He was also something of a snob, not wanting to get close to his classmates until he made sure their social status was up to his family's standards.

His father had told him, "Take care of your morals first, your health next, and finally your studies." After recovering from devastation over his father's death two years later, he doubled his activities. He did well in science, philosophy, and rhetoric courses but continued to struggle in Latin and Greek.

In 1880 he graduated Phi Beta Kappa, 22nd of 177 in his class. He entered Columbia Law School. He eventually became disenchanted with law. He dropped out of law school, saying, "I intend to be one of the governing class."

- twenty-seven -

He was born in Cincinnati, Ohio, in 1857.

In the hours after his birth, his mother had a fair prospect of milk and on the third day the boy had plenty, but a few days later, the infant's clamorous appetite necessitated a wet nurse to supplement his mother's milk supply.

Six days after his birth, his father proudly noted to a friend: the baby is fat and healthy.

At two months his mother recorded that he was very large for his age, and grows fat every day. Indeed, she noted with amazement and pride, he has such a large waist, that he cannot wear any of the dresses that we made with belts.

His parents admired his cherubic face, a solitary dimple in one cheek, his eyes deeply, darkly, beautifully blue.

He grew up in a home that was comfortable, with financial means ample but not excessive.

His father served as secretary of war and as attorney general under President Ulysses S. Grant.

At the age of seven he was reading, but his mother had to work with him in arithmetic and writing.

When he was eight he showed his first demonstration of leadership, as captain of the "Mt. Auburn crowd," the little group of Mt. Auburn boys of his age who made live worth living.

His parents reared him in the Unitarian faith.

From the start he was of that sturdy mold which gave promise of development into the tremendous frame of the full-grown man. He was a good play-fellow, a bit too slow-moving for a first class captain of baseball, but a master swimmer, and pioneer of the "plumping" game at marbles.

By the age of twelve, his last year in grammar school, he ranked first in his class, earning both his school's highest medal and his father's highest praise.

He attended a local dancing school where, by all accounts, he became an excellent dancer.

He struggled with his weight. A variety of explanations have been offered for his obesity. The trouble was food: He loved it, and the more food he could get, the more he loved it

He was possessed then of a curiosity that is abnormal with boys. It was aimed at the discovery of all that was concealed between the covers of his books. Ordinarily when a boy has that curiosity it results in his becoming an object of derision among his mates. It leads to the bandying of epithets like "milksop" and "sissy," which are fighting words wherever boyhood is human. But he was not of that kind. He was just as ready for a game as the next one, but when it was time to work he was for doing the work.

He devoured the newspapers, and hung fascinated over historical books.

He loved baseball, and he was a good second baseman and a power hitter. He studied at Woodward High School, a well-regarded private school in Cincinnati, graduating in 1874 second in the class with a four-year grade point average of 91.5 out of 100.

His personality made him a favorite everywhere. It was very hard to be near him without loving him.

He lived in constant fear of not meeting his parents' expectations.

No matter how well he performed, he was anxious about their approval.

Once, when his rank in class dropped from first or second down to fifth, his father was displeased and said, "Mediocrity will not do."

An attractive young man, quite agile for one with a heavy build, he appears not to have possessed a particularly precocious mind. He compensated for this by an unusual "ability to concentrate," balanced by a tendency to procrastinate. On the other hand, if attracted to a topic or assignment, he worked at it with a single-minded determination.

His native equipment was of a character to take him as far as he willed to go.

His hair was light and wavy.

His triple inheritance of brains, physique, and disposition began early to manifest itself. He liked to play, but he had no fear of work, or inclination to shirk it. These are all qualities he displayed in childhood.

They called him "Lubber" in those days because his movements had not the element of grace and activity which boys of less burly build possessed. He was indifferently "Lubber" or "Lub" until his increasing prowess at wrestling, and his developing mastery of his mates gradually overcame "Lubber."

Endowed by nature with great strength and extraordinary capacity for physical endurance, and pushed to the limit of studious application by a stern but wise father, he was forced to become the best possible exemplification of the old Yale ideal of the sound mind in the sound body.

When he entered Yale, he stood over six feet tall and weighed 225 pounds. To see his large bulk come solidly and fearlessly across the campus, one classmate enthused, is to take a fresh hold on life.

Unlike many of his classmates, he neither smoked nor drank more than an occasional glass of beer. He seems not to have enjoyed much of a social life while at Yale. He was selected for membership in Skull and Bones, a fraternity that included some of America's most famous men.

He seemed, like his father, to be headed for a career in law.

His tuition at Yale was $33 a year, and the students were required to attend religious services on a daily basis. He found the chapel seats unduly hard, the sermons dull. He once asked, "Why don't they try to make religion a little more attractive."

He served as the salutatorian for his class at commencement.

- twenty-eight -

When he was born on December 28, 1856, his birth was big news in the town of Staunton, Virginia.

He was his parents' third child and first son. He was born in the house that the First Presbyterian Church provided to his minister father.

His mother wrote to her father to say that he was "a fine healthy boy…and as fat as he can be. Everyone tells us he is a *beautiful* boy."

His father—outgoing, witty, and much given to puns—did not fit the prevalent stereotype of the stern minister. His father smoked cigars and pipes heavily, played billiards, dressed well, and took an occasional drink of Scotch whisky.

Before his first birthday, his family moved to Augusta, Georgia.

His first lasting memory from childhood went back to November 1860, just before his fourth birthday, hearing someone pass by and say that Mr. Lincoln was elected and there was to be a war.

His father asked him questions about what he saw. He said his father was the "best teacher I ever had."

His mother worried about him. He had stomach problems and bad colds. He also suffered from bad headaches, just as she did. His father fervently embraced the cause of the South and offered his church as the meeting place for the newly formed General Assembly of the Presbyterian Church of the Confederate States of American.

The war came home to his family when wounded Confederate soldiers began to arrive.

His mother could see that he was a slow learner.

He almost certainly saw and heard wounded and dying soldiers in the town and his father's church and prisoners of war in the churchyard.

Yet those sights and sounds did not seem to have affected him deeply. Nor did his boyhood experiences fill him with repugnance toward fighting or war. If the Civil War left a psychological imprint on him, it was buried so deep as to be imponderable.

Except for the war, he seems to have had a happy, healthy childhood. His older sisters reportedly adored him, and his mother unquestionably played the biggest role in his early life, while his father was often away.

At the end of the war, he watched a conquering army occupy his hometown, and he saw the captured Confederate president, Jefferson Davis, being transported to prison.

For him, probably the most important effect of the war was a delay in starting school.

As an urban minister's son, he had a more sheltered upbringing than did the mischief-filled, rough-and-tumble southern white boys depicted in Mark Twain's stories. Yet like Tom Sawyer, he had a rich, elaborate fantasy life and enjoyed a certain amount of mischief. He once recalled that he liked cockfighting, evidently using the family rooster.

One of his friends in Augusta later recalled him as "a dignified boy" who on horseback was "a conservative rider...very careful and very orderly."

One day he heard the circus was in town. He and his friends skipped school, and they spent the day following the elephant

113

parading around the city.

In his youth he played baseball.

He and his friends organized a baseball club after the war, and the same friend remembered him as "not active or especially strong, although his figure was well-knit and he was what you would call a 'stocky' boy."

He wrote a constitution with rules for their baseball club. If the boys didn't follow the rules, he made them pay a fine. If a boy swore, he had them put five cents in a jar. He liked to have other boys obey his rules.

He did not appear at first to be very bright. He was slow in learning to read. He had not learned his letters until he was nine, and he did not read comfortably until he was twelve. His difficulty reading most likely stemmed from some physical issue. His vision may have contributed to the problem.

His delayed intellectual development may be attributed to the Civil War, or, as modern science suggests, his delay could have resulted from an undiagnosed learning disability: dyslexia.
Handwriting didn't come easy to him, either. He practiced and practiced. He wrote his name again and again until he liked the way it looked. Then he found out about shorthand. Shorthand symbols made it easier for him to write faster, so he no longer got behind taking notes in class.

From his father he learned to set his goals high and never to accept second best from himself. When he wrote essays to please his father, they always had to be revised, no matter how carefully they were done in the first place.

He never smoked.

He often shadowed and assisted his father in pastoral meetings by helping to record the minutes. This experience confirmed in his young mind that he did not want to work directly in the church. He was sure that he did not want to follow in his father's footsteps.

In Augusta, he went to an all-boys private school.

Without thinking about it, he absorbed the values and attitudes of his religion.

His eventual decision to leave the South was the culmination of a slow maturation process that began in 1873 when he first left home for college.

Homesick at Davidson College (North Carolina), he kept a list of letters received from and sent to members of his family. Yet even as he suffered the show of separation, he was beginning to move beyond his family circle and to build a life of his own. Despite recurring illnesses, which were probably psychosomatic in part, he passed his courses and found time to participate in a debating club, for which he wrote a new constitution.

He played second base for his freshman baseball team. But instead of returning to Davidson for his sophomore year, he studied at home during the 1874-1875 school year in preparation for a new institution, the College of New Jersey, at Princeton.

The Princeton he entered in 1875 was beginning to change from a quiet country college to one of the most notable institutions of the country.

Princeton's blend of secularism and religious idealism suited him perfectly, and he quickly made friends with other young men who shared his vision of a literate, service-oriented elite reforming American political life.

He never had any real enthusiasm for law but recognized that it was a traditional route to political office.

In college he earned good grades in Latin and Greek and French and he used German in his scholarly work, although he never became fluent in any foreign language.

The classroom itself wasn't what captivated him and grabbed his attention during his undergraduate years at Princeton. He became fascinated with how his mind worked rather than what could be stuffed into it in a classroom.

He admired scholars for their imagination, expression, and intellect.

He had a busy social life at Princeton. He joined an eating club called the Alligators. He was also the managing editor of Princeton's campus newspaper, *The Princetonian*. As an upperclassman, he lived in Witherspoon Hall, the most popular dorm on campus.

Throughout his years at Princeton, his interest in politics grew. He published his ideas even as an undergraduate.

- twenty-nine -

His life began as the Civil War was ending, on November 2, 1865.

He was the oldest of eight children.

His father was a Union soldier—a fifer who had once shaken President Lincoln's hand at the White House. His mother taught him many poems, which he proudly recited for relatives and family friends.

By age four he was reading. A born talker, he was encouraged to enter his first oratorical contest at age four. A year later, when he heard bells toll, he piped up, "They're ringing for (George) Washington. Some day they will ring for me."

His mother repeatedly predicted that he would become President.

He had his father's musical ear and talent, which could be heard by all the neighboring farmers when he was given a cornet at age nine.

His boyhood was not materially different from that of other boys of the community. He simply made the most of his limited opportunities. He worked, obtained an education, and his life demonstrated his superior industry, capability, intelligence and leadership. He was worthy. He was just plain folks.

His formal education began in a one-room schoolhouse, where he studied reading, writing, spelling, mathematics, history, and geography.

His first heroes were Napoleon Bonaparte and Alexander Hamilton.

He was regarded as non-white at a time when racial prejudice was the norm.

When he was a small boy he used to get broom stalks from the farmers and then make the brooms. When he had done ten or a dozen he would start out to peddle them. He also earned a dollar now and then playing in the Caledonia village band, and later was a member of the Marion band when it won a prize at a tournament.

Growing up in a rural farming community, he and his friends spent the summers fishing and swimming. During the fall, he went out to gather hickory nuts and butternuts for his family to enjoy.

He liked sports and enjoyed being outdoors with his friends. His mother, however, placed more emphasis on education. She made sure that he did not miss school and that he spent enough time studying.

His grandfather had built the one-room schoolhouse for the area's children.

He was a good boy in school. Of course he used to get into mischief and did tricks like all other boys, but he was so honest that he always got caught. He was always honest and truthful.

When he started school at Blooming Grove he was a boy rather large for his age and was noticeable for his clean ways, manly spirit and straightforwardness. His voice was strong, well-toned and full. He took all his studies seriously but performed his tasks with astonishing ease.

Sometimes going to school or even just being around other children turned into an unpleasant experience for him. Some children called him names, using racial slurs. Their taunts stemmed from a rumor that had circulated around town for years—that his family had an African American somewhere in the family tree. The rumor was fueled by the fact that he and some of his siblings had dark eyes and hair and olive skin. Some people in town said that his great-grandfather had come from the West Indies.

They always called him "Nigger," because he looked so black when wet with water after they went swimming together.

More than anything else, he wanted to belong. He reacted to slurs by trying harder than ever to fit in and be popular. He worked on making himself so agreeable that no one would exclude him. He learned how to please and get along with those around him and how to be a good friend. He made a point of never losing his temper and took pride in being a good sport.

As a result, he became well liked. But he paid a price for this acceptance. Pressured by the need to please other people and conform to their views, he never developed a firm sense of self-confidence or decisiveness.

His parents wanted more for themselves and their children than life on the farm, so they both began to study medicine with local doctors. His father completed his medical training and soon has his own small practice, while his mother developed an active rural and town practice as a midwife.

He had a good home, devoted parents and the encouragement of brothers and sisters, but like the average American parents, his were in only moderate financial circumstances and it was necessary for him, even in his school days, to rustle about for odd jobs, to provide spending change.

The summer months of his youth were spent in doing chores, and their category included: Painting barns, fences and sheds, chopping wood, laying ties with a gang on a new railway, and much hard labor as a farmer.

Caledonia is the town where he first got printer's ink on his fingers. He was a "devil"—as print shop apprentices are known—in the office of the *Caledonia Argus*, and he learned how to stick type, feed press, make up forms and wash rollers. We rode a mule to the print shop and set type in his bare feet.

At fourteen years of age, in the fall of 1879, he entered Ohio Central College, located in Iberia, Ohio. He was a gangling but strong fellow, already six feet tall, with an olive complexion, blue eyes, and wavy black hair. He worked his way through college by painting houses and barns, and, during the summers, doing heavy construction work on railroad gradings. He helped with the construction work on the Ohio Central Railroad.

As a college student he most enjoyed his courses in literature and philosophy. Other subjects were easily ignored until the last minute, for he was good at cramming. Foreshadowing his business career, he launched a college newspaper with his roommate during their last year, called the *Iberia Spectator*.

According to his roommate, he knew every pretty girl within five miles of the college.

He visited his mother every Sunday to bring her a bouquet of flowers. When he was later too far away to visit, he arranged to have flowers delivered, a practice that continued throughout her lifetime.

Upon his graduation in 1882, at seventeen years of age, he moved back home. He had no idea what to do with his life. The only job that he could get was as a teacher in the local colored school.

When he was nineteen years of age, he moved with his family to Marion. He tried his hand at selling fire and life insurance. He met with unusual success. He started after that business as the agent of three insurance companies. Strange to say, one of his earliest clients was his future father-in-law, Amos Kling, though he had not then met his daughter.

- thirty -

He was born in Plymouth Notch, Windsor County, Vermont, on July 4, 1872, the only U.S. President to be born on Independence Day.

The house in which he was born was a five-room story-and-a-half cottage to which were attached a post office and general store; his father's store.

A horrible shyness possessed him, possessed him from his earliest days and never left him.

Two days after he was two months old, his father was elected to the state legislature. His father was at times a Justice of the Peace and always had a commission as notary republic.

His father paid $40 a year rent for the country store and turned over $10,000 a year in goods. But his parents would not charge high prices to their neighbors; that might turn away business.

When he was three, his grandfather took him up to Montpelier to visit his father the lawmaker and placed the boy in the governor's chair, hewn from timbers of the USS *Constitution*, known as Old Ironsides, one of the United States' first ships.

He was a red-haired boy.

He was not an especially fast runner, he was not especially comfortable with a ball, and he was certainly not comfortable dancing. So the boy in his way was more than a bit shy. The villagers noticed early that he was always quiet; when someone played the violin, he would not dance, but was always observant.

When he was a little fellow, he would go into a panic if he heard strange voices in the house. He felt he just couldn't meet people. He was almost ten before he realized he couldn't go on that way.

His school year began in May and ended in February; the roads were too muddy and the sugaring was too demanding for pupils to take time to go to school in the spring.

He was not an inquisitive boy, one of his teachers recalled.

He did well enough in his studies; he even pulled pranks. He not only liked practical jokes but saw that others liked them.

His mother loved literature and poetry and shared this love with her son and daughter. He grew up with the works of great writers such as William Shakespeare, Scottish novelist Walter Scott, and the poet Alfred, Lord Tennyson.

His favorite avocation was reading.

Even when small, he saw politics first hand: at town meetings, it was his father who spoke. He sold apples and popcorn at the meetings, as his father had before him.

His grandmother wove fabric, and the women in the family made patchwork quilts. At age ten he stitched a quilt top of Tumbling Blocks, a dauntingly sophisticated pattern.
His father noted with relief that he was diligent at sugaring and much later told a reporter proudly that his son could get "more sap out of a maple tree than the other boys around here."

He could whittle and he knew every tree, the mountain ash, the plum, and the lilac bush around the house.

He was not always patient.

His mother was chronically ill and died, perhaps from tuberculosis, when he was twelve years old.

His mother's death hit him hard. He grew taller, thin and

quiet. People wondered if he too might be susceptible to consumption; they agreed that his small features and pale looks recalled his mother and fitted the general stereotype of the consumptive.

He attended Black River Academy. In his first terms, he took algebra, grammar, and civil government. His grade average was 83.8.

While in theory he was always urged to work and to save, in practice he was permitted to do his share of playing and wasting.

Heartbreak in childhood and in youth makes deep changes in the channel of one's life and destiny, and those who knew him best found in him a tenderness and an unusual capacity for sentimentality, the more powerful because it was repressed.

As a little fellow, he played with his grandfather, a tall, gaunt Yankee who stood better than six feet high and was always running for office.

He went to Sunday school through his childhood and well into his youth.

No course in manual training set down by a wise pedagogue could have done more to make a handy youth out of a New England visionary than the training he, as a child and boy, had in the Notch at Plymouth. His grandfather initiated him in the lore of horses and dogs, chickens and sheep, cattle and pigs.

He liked the circus. But his father said of him that as a child he did not care for play, and he himself repeatedly admitted the same thing with perfect frankness.

He made kites, cut out arrows from the pine and ash, made bows from the hickory, had a pocket-knife before he could read, and used the adz before he knew the multiplication tables.

He was never quite the same after his mother died, one of

several deaths that affected him while growing up.

He was not particularly a good boy, nor did he work harder than other boys, nor was he brighter. He was just an average country boy in a New England farm village who skated on the ponds in winter and swam in them in the summer. He hunted, trapped in the woods and brush, fished in streams, and learned to love the gifts the seasons brought, the field flowers, the distant velvety hills all green with spruce in winter and aglow with the new foliage, the hickory, the ash, the maple, the elm in spring. He had a calico horse which was his delight. This gave him distinction. It was marked like a circus horse and he could ride standing.

He was never of large stature, though healthy and able to do his share of manual work. He was never a youthful prodigy. In a school of about thirty, he was among the first half dozen. He was methodical, faithful, honest and punctual, never tardy, never much ahead of time.

He was not mischievous or adventuresome, and was uncomfortable in large groups.

He liked to ride his horse alone through the Vermont forests.

He carried a portrait of his mother wherever he went.

The boys at Black River Academy had to wear coats, ties, and stiff collars, but he went overboard, wearing a derby, a starched dickey, and carrying a cane, perhaps in order to draw attention to himself. Not only did he become something of a fashion plate, but he also started a small business of selling mail order jewelry to his classmates.

As a freshman at Amherst, he boarded at Trott's on South Pleasant Street, ten minutes from the college, farther away than most students. He was at Amherst during one the nation's most severe economic depressions.

In his junior year in college, he told a friend that he might return to his hometown and become a storekeeper like his father, and spend his spare time reading. He did not attend school to better himself socially or financially.

He did not visit Boston until he was a college upperclassman.

There was a word, he learned, for a man who was left out without a fraternity: they called such a man an ouden, from the Greek for "nothing."

He was never a joiner.

He finally received a firm invitation to join Phi Gamma Delta in his last year at Amherst. He accepted quite willingly. But he did not move into the fraternity house; he remained a border for the remainder of his college career.

Traditionally, the young men of Amherst College dated young women from the nearby colleges of Smith and Mount Holyoke, but he had no dates.

At his father's urging, he moved to Northampton, Massachusetts after graduating to take up the practice of law.

- thirty-one -

He was the last president to be born (August 10, 1874) and raised in a frontier environment and the first born west of the Mississippi River.

His father was a hard-working blacksmith. He loved to watch his father shape horseshoes and other metalworks.

His mother was an itinerant, unpaid Quaker minister. His father was also a fervent Quaker. All of his grandparents were Quakers, and Quaker records run back a long time.

His home life was happy. His family lived in a small cottage with handcrafted furniture made by his father and rugs pieced together by his mother.

The first six years of his life were happy and carefree. His boyhood had much in common with Huckleberry Finn's.

Amiably rambunctious, he swam at a muddy swimming hole during the summer and coasted down a sledding hill during cold, windy winters on the plains.

There was the traditional "ol' swimmin' hole" at West Branch— it's merely a mud bank now—but he and the "gang" usually could be found there at least an hour a day between June and October. He caught sunfish and damned small streams to trap trout. Some of his playmates were Indians who taught him frontier lore.

He enjoyed fascinating friendships with Indian boys. He watched the little braves snare rabbits and ground squirrels; he fished beside them with a bent pin. He made his own childish efforts to draw the hickory bow; he stood in a state of exalted admiration while they cooked their prey on a lid of a tin can. This halcyon of genuine boy-scouting marked his tastes and character.

He went to school, of course, and while his primary teacher, Mrs. J. K. Carran, avers he "was a mighty good boy" and "quick to learn," she does not contend that he especially excelled in his studies. A mediocre student, weak in English, who excelled in math, he enjoyed his time outdoors at recess.

The first blow came when his father died at thirty-four of a heart attack when he was six. Two years later, his mother succumbed to pneumonia after a frigid walk from a neighboring town where she had preached.

He was sent to live with his Uncle, who recently lost his son. He made the long train trek to Newberg, Oregon alone.

He was orphaned at nine and was raised on the cusp of the frontier,

As the train chugged westward, he saw for the first time the rugged terrain of the western landscape. Some geological formations—such as Castle Rock in Colorado and the Devil's Slide in California—enthralled him.

His childhood seems singularly free of political memories. None of those who remember him as a youth can recall his taking part in any political discussions—although he once carried a torch in a parade to boost the candidacy of Garfield.

He demonstrated an early interest in geology by picking fossilized rocks from the gravel along the railroad tracks and labelling them.

His natural sense of aloofness probably was intensified when he moved to Oregon.

It is the problem of the psychiatrist rather than the biographer to determine to what extent his nature was permanently warped by his tragic childhood, but it must be fairly obvious even to the most unreflecting reader that it was altered in some essential respects. Until his father's death he had a normal, happy childhood; after his father's death he was shamefully neglected—not that he was not sufficiently clothed, fed, schooled, and sheltered; but that in the sense he was lonely, misunderstood, resentful, and actually starved for affection.

But he was by no means a neglected orphan.

The few early photographs still extant depict him as chubby, round-faced, with stubborn unruly hair, and usually smiling.

He was subjected to such sudden variations in affectional heat and cold that he withdrew into himself.

As he was shunted from here to there—among aunts and uncles—each new group of guardians probably quizzed him mercilessly about his family affairs and pried into every crevice of his being in search of fresh gossip.

Usually he earned his keep, and the ordinary routine meant milking, slopping the hogs, cleaning out stables, hoeing potatoes and corn, creeping on all fours for hours at a stretch while weeding root crops. But there is no evidence that he complained, shirked his tasks, or thought himself particularly abused.

It was not the hard labor that he minded so much as the almost complete absence of family life, and with that intimate parental care which every child craves and needs for its normal development.

After a breakfast of corn mush and milk, he chopped wood and hauled water to the cottage from an outside pump. In the winter, he grabbed his homemade sled and headed for snow-covered Cook's Hill.

When he was fifteen, his Uncle John moved the family to nearby Salem, the capital city of Oregon. Instead of attending high school, he was employed as an office boy in his uncle's company. Running errands did not interest him. Always curious and driven, he used his spare time in the office to help the firm's accountant and secretary. From them, he learned the basics of bookkeeping and how to type.

At night he took classes at business school.

After two years working as an office boy, he was ready to continue his education beyond night school. His relatives wanted him to attend a Quaker college and offered to him a scholarship. But he had other ideas. He wanted to study mechanical engineering. From a Quaker friend, he learned about Stanford University, a new college in California that needed students and did not charge tuition.

Almost everyone who came to know him at Stanford was impressed with his capacity for work and his talent for organizing and planning projects.

By his own admission, his interest at Stanford centered on his extracurricular activities rather than on academics, in which he was usually average.

While there was no charge for tuition at Stanford, he had to pay for his room, board, books, and other expenses. Looking to earn money, he identified the needs of his fellow students and launched some successful enterprises to meet those needs. He ran a laundry service and a concert series and organized a campus paper route. He eventually sold the laundry business to another student for a profit.

- thirty-two -

When the boy was born on January 30, 1882, he was blue and not breathing.

But the doctor performed mouth-to-mouth resuscitation and he came around.

"He weighs ten pounds without clothes," his father wrote.

For the next two months the baby went unnamed.

His first words were "Mama" and "Papa," apparently in that order; he added "Mamie" for the nurse who tended to the less appealing aspects of child rearing.

Weaned at twelve months, walking at sixteen, he was neither precocious nor slow.

By his second Christmas, he would stand next to his Mamma, handing out toys to the children of their servants. As for his own gifts, all he had to say was that he wanted something and it was given to him.

As an only child, his life revolved around gaining the attention and admiration of adults, especially his parents. He was the center of the universe, as far as he knew. No siblings intruded upon his consciousness.

He had long blond hair and wore dresses with fancy lace collars until he was almost six.

At six he attended an impromptu kindergarten on a neighboring estate. Then he began working with a series of governesses and tutors at home.

From his formative years, he loved to be at the center of attention and believed that he was destined to perform great deeds in the service of humanity. He developed stoical traits of character that stressed discipline, responsibility, and trust in his own judgment.

He learned how to set firm priorities, to give others no more than what he considered their due, to keep his inner thoughts private, and to deflect external pressure with winning charm and subtle persuasion so as not to be swayed from his course.

He was raised to believe that the presidency was entirely within reach, should he be interested.

He was something of a mama's boy. He was the apple of his mother's eye and loved her very much, even when she was bossy.

He drank out of a fancy silver cup from Russia. After all, he was the ultimate rich kid.

Though he could be perfectly content on his own, reading or pasting items into his beloved stamp albums, he also loved getting to know people, and enjoyed true conversation.

Not until he was nearly eight did he wear pants in the form of miniature sailor suits purchased from London.

He seemed to be missing the normal emotional equipment that produces worry. In keeping with upper-class custom in America at the time, he saw more of the help than he did of his parents. He was almost nine and had never taken a bath by himself before.

In the winter he went on sleigh rides or sledded full speed down snowy hills. He was happy exploring the woods and fields.

He did not go to school. He was taught at home by tutors until he was thirteen. He grew up with few playmates and little company beyond parents and tutors.

He rarely clashed with other children, for he spent most of his time among adults.

His mind was continually challenged. While public school children his age were learning their ABCs in English, he was mastering them simultaneously in French and German.

He already possessed an uncanny ability to assimilate what he observed. He learned by doing.

He developed lifelong interests in stamp collecting, geography, and history, which later provided him an independent vision of the world.

His ever-growing list of eclectic interests—stamps, stuffed birds, Navy ships, rare books—later contributed to his reputation as a dilettante.

In one respect he may have been cared for *too* well. Most children in the nineteenth century, like most children for the millennia past, were exposed to all manner of microbes at an early age; many died of infant and childhood illnesses, but those who survived developed robust immune systems, able to cope with the mundane infections they subsequently encountered. He, by virtue of his comparative isolation, missed out on some of this tempering.

Like his parents, he took pride in his Protestant heritage.

But he wasn't a regular churchgoer. In his youth and young adulthood he had often spent Sundays on the golf course.

Fire was the only thing he truly feared in life.

He loved the water. On his mother's side he was the scion of an old seafaring family. He had grown up sailing small boats on the mid-Hudson and among rocky islands of the northern seacoast. As a teenager his great ambition had been to attend the U.S. Naval academy and command ships at sea.

The world afforded ceaseless entertainment: pony and buggy and sleigh rides, tobogganing on the slopes above the Hudson, journeys by train and steamship to exciting cities and countries, stays in fine hotels and fancy houses.

The extensive travel that he did with his parents—he went to Europe eight times in his first fourteen years—exposed him to a wider range of experience than most boys his age. He was small for his age—five feet three, 105 pounds—but his physical growth had yet to begin.

All in all he looked forward to entering Groton—two years late, as it were, most boys entering at the age of twelve. For fourteen years he had been the center of attention of two doting parents. Now he was one of 110 adolescent boys living in an almost monastic setting. If he was concerned, he did not show it. "I am getting on finely both mentally and physically," he reported in his first letter home.

After years of his family's adoration, he faced merciless adolescent peers, some of whom called him the "feather duster" (after his initials) because they found him shallow and conceited.

He didn't sound like a New Yorker, not even a Hudson Valley Knickerbocker. He didn't sound like a New Englander, despite the summers spent with his maternal grandparents. He did sound rich, but this was as much a matter of tone and timbre— the self-confidence of one who expected the world to treat him well—as of pronunciation.

He sounded vaguely British, which made sense in terms of his upbringing.

His summers abroad had left him with an accent that the other boys considered "too English."

He didn't exactly ignore his studies.

His courses included a full round of English, history, and government, as well as the odd philosophy and fine arts class. He passed them all, without distinction.

He excelled only at Latin.

Because he had taken several college-level courses at Groton, he completed the requirements for his bachelor's degree by the end of his third year. But he didn't dream for a minute of skipping his fourth year, which he expected to be his time of social glory.

At Harvard he remained outside the "in" groups. He edited his university's newspaper.

He seemed supernaturally capable of tuning to the frequency of other people. Like a chameleon he changed colors with the person he was talking with.

He stood an inch or so above six feet but somehow seemed larger, perhaps because of his especially large head and jutting chin and his habit of quick and incessant movement.

While he was at Harvard he certainly didn't appear to dwell on his exclusion from the single stuffiest of the clubs but rather made do quite well with others. He was chosen for Alpha Delta Phi, known as the "Fly Club," of which he became the librarian; the Institute of 1770; the Signet Literary Society; the Memorial Society, which served as keeper of the Harvard history and traditions; and Hasty Pudding, the student theatrical group.

He possessed one of the great names in American politics. He planned to do a great deal.

- thirty-three -

In a quandary over a middle name,
his parents were undecided whether to
honor her father or his—in the end they
compromised with the letter S.

It could be taken to stand for both of his grandfathers: Solomon
or Shipp, but it actually stood for nothing, a practice not
unknown among the Scotch-Irish, even for first names.

He was born on May 8, 1884 in Lamar, Missouri, and in 1890 his
family moved to Independence, Missouri.

His earliest memory, interestingly, was of laughter. He was
chasing a frog around the yard, laughing every time it jumped.
The second memory was of his mother, for fun, dropping him
from an upstairs window into the outstretched arms of his very
large Uncle Harry, who was to be a particular favorite from then
on.

He had a black-and-tan dog of uncertain ancestry called Tandy
and a cat named Bob. He liked to say in later years that he had
the happiest childhood imaginable.

By nature he was a quiet boy.

A few miles beyond his parents farm with its 600 acres was a
second farm owned by his Grandpa, this with nearly 1,000 acres.

His Grandpa was a big, impressive looking man who had
strong hands and flowing white beard. His Grandpa was one
of the first settlers to arrive in Jackson County, Missouri, and
was considered a very important man, so he was always asked
to judge the harness races at the fair. That meant he and his

Grandpa would sit in the judges' stand, where they had the best view. He felt really special doing that, but he never acted special around other kids. He loved his Grandpa dearly, and he always tried to please him.

He had a swing under an old elm close to the house and another swing indoors in the front hall for rainy days.

It was Mamma, he decided, who understood him best. She was brighter than anyone, he thought, and cared most about his well-being.

His father presented him with a black Shetland pony and a new saddle. With the pony on a lead, he rode beside his father as he made the rounds on the farm.

There was always an abundance of food on the farm—dried apples, peaches, candy and nuts of all kinds, wonder cookies, pies, corn pudding, roasting meats in the summer, peach butter, apple butter, grape butter, jellies and preserves.

On the summer day when his Grandpa died, he rushed to the bed to pull at the old man's beard, trying desperately to wake him.

Climbing on a chair, in an attempt to comb his hair in front of a mirror, he toppled over backward and broke his collarbone.

Once, he would have choked on a peach stone had his mother not responded in a flash and decisively, pushing the stone down his throat with her finger instead of trying to pull it out.
When he was growing up it occurred to him to watch the people around him to find out what they thought and what pleased them most. He used to watch his father and mother closely to learn what he could do to please them, just as he did with his schoolteachers and playmates. It was thus, but getting along with people, he discovered, that he could nearly always get what he wanted.

He was not dedicated to himself; he had no feelings of self-importance.

Though he had been badly handicapped by poor eyesight all along—"blind as a mole," in his words—no one seems to have noticed until the night of a July Fourth fireworks when they saw him responding more to the sound of the skyrockets than to the spectacle overhead. The Kansas City optometrist diagnosed his rare malformation called "flat eyeballs" (hypermetropia, which meant he was farsighted). He got a pair of double-strength, wire-rimmed spectacles at a cost of $10.

He was an exceptionally alert, good little boy of sunny disposition. He appears to have liked school from the start. His favorite subject was history. He realized history had some valuable lessons to teach. By his graduation from grammar school, he had read all the books in the Independence Public Library and gone through the family Bible three times.

His favorite author was Mark Twain.

In Sunday school he met Bess Wallace. They went to different grammar schools for a while, but they met again in the fifth grade. It took him months to get up the nerve to speak to her.
For several years, he took piano lessons on a regular basis, once or twice a week. He arose early and practiced two hours before school. He could play at sight on the piano any piece set before him, seemingly as well as if he had drilled for the occasion. He could instantly improvise any style of music desired and change off to other styles as fast as they were suggested.

He always gave the impression that he was not very serious about playing the piano, and sometimes he passed it off with a joke. On occasion he related that while in high school he began to fear playing was a sissy occupation, and so quit.

When old enough to get a job outside the house, he worked in Clinton's Drugstore. He worked there from seven o'clock until schooltime and after school from four to ten. He dispensed ice cream from behind the soda foundation, carried out the trash, and swept the store. With his first week's pay—three silver dollars—he bought a present for his mother and tried to give the rest to his father, who would not take it.

In 1900, when he was sixteen, he attended the Democratic National Convention in Kansas City with his father.

His father held various jobs, from farmer to night watchman, depending on his financial situation and geographic location. His mother was supportive and strong-minded.

His father ran into financial trouble and could not afford to send him to college.

When he graduated from high school in 1901, he wanted to attend the United States Military Academy, but poor eyesight barred him from West Point.

After high school, he worked first for the Santa Fe Railroad and then as a bank clerk. He really liked living on his own in a boarding house in Kansas City.

He served in the Missouri National Guard during World War I.

His unit was called into duty in 1917. He believed it was the duty of the United States to help Great Britain, France, and Russia fight Germany and its allies, known as the Central Powers. He left for France in April 1918 and served there as an officer. His troops included tough men who liked to look for trouble, but they obeyed him.

- thirty-four -

He had a late-nineteenth century,
Tom Sawyer-like upbringing—save for
the absence of the river and Huck Finn.

He was born on October 14, 1890, in a small rented frame
house, not much more than a shack, beside the railroad tracks
in Denison, Texas.

In 1891, the family moved to Abeline, Kansas. His father had
in his pocket the sum total of his capital, $10. His father, a
creamery worker, read the Bible aloud to his family, and both
parents preached "getting ahead." His family was Mennonite,
fundamentalists in their religion, and pacifists.

He had five brothers. The family was respected around town,
but they were in no way prominent. His parents were frugal
out of necessity, but they were proud and ambitious, if not for
themselves, then for their sons.

He attended Lincoln elementary school, directly across the
street from his home.

His home life revolved around worship. Every day, morning
and night, the family members got down on their knees to pray.
His father read from the Bible before meals, then asked for
a blessing. After the meals, the boys washed the dishes, then
gathered around their father for Bible reading.

On Halloween night, 1900, his parents gave his two older brothers
permission to go "trick or treating." He begged, pleaded, and
argued to be allowed to go along, but his parents insisted that
he was too young. Anger overwhelmed him. He rushed outside
and began pounding the trunk of an apple tree with his bare

fists. Finally his father grabbed him by the shoulders and shook him until he gained some control over himself. He went to his bed and cried into his pillow for an hour, out of resentment and rage. His mother came into the room and sat beside him. She took up his hands, putting salve on them and then bandages. After what seemed to him to be a long time, she said, "He that conquereth his own soul is greater than he who taketh a city."

He received decent grades in school, discovered an early interest in military history, and displayed leadership qualities in organizing athletic and other outdoor events—becoming as a youngster what he remained for life, an able book on camping trips.

He performed well enough in class, gathered quite a few demerits for disciplinary offenses, and, as a yearling (which is what West Point calls sophomores) showed signs that he was about to become a star running back on the football team. A knee injury cut short his gridiron career, whereupon he became such a keen student of the game that he was asked to coach the junior varsity. A turn as a cheerleader gave him valuable experience in public experiences.

He was a popular boy, well known for his curiosity, his fun-loving ways, his big smile, and his energy. But he had a terrible temper. Anger would possess him, take complete control, make him oblivious to anything else. The adrenalin rushed through his body, raising the hair on the back of his neck, turning his face a bright beet-red.

Spelling contests aroused in him his competitive drive and his hatred of careless mistakes—he (later) became a self-confessed martinet on the subject of orthography.

Arithmetic appealed to him because it was logical and straightforward—an answer was either right or wrong. His best grades were in English and history. The subject that really excited him, however, was one that he pursued on his own, military history. He became so engrossed in it, in fact, that he neglected his chores and his schoolwork. He became a student of the American Revolution—George Washington excited his admiration.

His first hero was Hannibal.

During his freshman year in high school, he fell and scraped his knee. His only thought was for his ruined brand-new pants, which he had bought with his own earnings. Since there was no bleeding, he went to school the next day. Infection set in, however, and that evening he fell into a delirium on the sofa in the front room. His parents called in a doctor, but despite his treatment, the infection began spreading. For the next two weeks, he slipped into and out of coma. The infection spread and crept up his leg toward his abdomen. His doctor called in a specialist from Topeka, and they both agreed that only amputation would save his life. During one of his conscious moments, he heard his parents discussing amputation. "You are not going to cut off that leg," he said quietly but firmly. At the end of the second week, the infection began to recede, the fever left his body. After a two-month convalescence, which caused him to have to repeat his freshman year, he recovered completely.

He took up gymnastics and learned to chin himself five times using only his right hand, and three times with only his left.

During his high school years his interests were, in order of importance, sports, work, studies, and girls. He was shy around the girls and in any case wanted to impress his male classmates as a regular fellow, just one of the gang. He was careless of his dress, his hair was usually uncombed, and he was a terrible dancer on the few occasions he tried the dance floor.

He talked history to his classmates so frequently that his senior yearbook predicted that he would become a professor of history at Yale.

He excelled at high school sports, showing his competitive spirit at a young age. He gained the attention of a few colleges, but he had no interest. However, he received a letter of acceptance to West Point Military Academy.

There is no evidence he fretted about his parents' pacifist convictions. When he left for the Academy, his mother saw him off from the front porch.

His principal vices were cigarette smoking and poker—both of which were forbidden at West Point. His vocabulary was punctuated with profanity that would make a mule skinner blush. He had a logical mind, a retentive memory, and a natural gift for writing clear, effective prose. During his first two years at the academy he played incessantly and kept a book in which he recorded his classmates IOUs to be paid after graduation.

Had it not been for athletics it is questionable whether he would have completed his four years at West Point. He was the first cadet on the field for football practice and the very last to leave. His enthusiasm for the game exceeded his abilities. He was just another average chap. He was a capable player, but just another player. Although he was never a player of the first rank, he made up in dedication and enthusiasm what he lacked in size and talent. Competitiveness, teamwork, and the pursuit of a common goal were imprinted as indelibly on his character as was the warrior ethic on men such as Patton and MacArthur.

He was not thirsting for glory, but he understood the career he had embarked upon. He had the priceless ability to make anyone he met feel that he had a genuine interest in him and in his ideas.

- thirty-five -

He was born in Brookline, Massachusetts, on May 29, 1917.

His father was a businessman/politician and his mother was a philanthropist/socialite.

He was the second oldest. But a more important part of his youth—and indeed of much of his life—was the long history of illness that began shortly after birth.

He was restless and fitful even as a baby, had trouble digesting milk, and suffered frequent stomach aches.

By the time he was three, he had experienced scarlet fever, causing his mother "frantic terror" and leading his father to spend hours praying (uncharacteristically) in the Catholic Church, which he rarely attended.

He was a funny little boy, and he said things in such an original, vivid way. His shirt never seemed to stay in his trousers, nor would his collar stay down.

Though he'd survived his bout with scarlet fever, he remained frail, skinny, and subject to almost continual illness.

When he is only six years old, he observed his grandfather campaigning for governor, a memory that stuck with him for life.

He'd inherited his father's sandy hair, bluish eyes, and squarish face; but the jaw, with its wide mouth and prominent teeth, belonged to his mother, as did his cooler temperament. His ears stuck out a little bit and his hair wouldn't stay put, and all that added to an elfin quality, full of energy when he wasn't ill and full of charm and imagination. And surprises—for he thought his own thoughts, did things his own way, and somehow just didn't fit any pattern.

X-rays showed no pathology in his knees, and so his doctor attributed his difficulties to growing pains and recommended exercises and "built-up" shoes.

His father, though absent much of the time, was at least an occasional father.

Within the somewhat philistine, regimented clan, he was the bookworm.

He was under the shadow of his older brother who was the recipient of his father's greatest hopes. Living in the shadow of his older brother was difficult.

His older brother, bigger and stronger than him, bullied him, and fights between the two—often fierce wrestling matches—terrified their younger brother and sisters. He particularly remembered a bicycle race that his older brother suggested. They sped around the block in opposite directions, meeting head-on in front of their house. Never willing to concede superiority to the other, neither backed off from a collision that left his brother unhurt and him nursing twenty-eight stitches.

An IQ of 119 and strong scores on the English and algebra parts of his Choate entrance exams had helped ease his admission.

English, in which he was required to read his favorite author, Sir Walter Scott, remained his best subject, earning him a 95 grade, followed by 93 in math, 80 in history, and 68 in Latin (he would never do well in languages).

He had mumps and the doctor thought it was a cold.

This frightening illness was followed by other debilitating diseases (chicken pox, ear infections, and undiagnosed stomach, intestinal, and other ailments that made it difficult for him to eat and sometimes left him so weak that he could hardly stand). Sickness plagued him into adolescence and beyond, baffling his doctors, his family.

More and more he sought refuge in the infirmary.

His letters from boarding school were always filled with references to his younger siblings, for they looked up to him. He was often homesick and wrote to his mother and father to send him newspapers and golf balls.

He was also the family joker: witty, irresponsible, irreverent, careless, and tardy, refusing to conform like other children to his mother's pathetic preoccupation with manners.

His illnesses inevitably affected his schooling.

"He was sick all the time," one of his friends recalled, "and his old man could be an asshole around his kids."

He was constantly reprimanded by his teachers and the headmaster, who considered him "one of the most undependable boys" in his grade. He lacked "application." He was "careless" with work. He was notoriously "casual and disorderly" in a school committed to order.

Everyone agreed that he was intelligent, but that made his scholarly "mediocrity" all the more damning.

He had a delightful sense of humor always...he was a very likable person, very lovable. It was not surprising that his jokes were often dark, because his health continued to deteriorate.

He spent weeks at the Mayo Clinic, where he submitted to what seemed endless, humiliating tests.

Partly to compensate for his inability to thrive in sports or academics, he developed a new sexual prowess that lasted through the rest of his life.

Careless and untidy, yet he had a winning way with friends and young women.

Playing football on the school's "small team," he displayed quickness and spunk and performed well enough to warrant mention in the school's newspaper.

At choir practice he thought he sounded increasingly like the family's pet dog.

Mysteriously, he was often tired and sick and wasn't gaining weight. He had hives, and complained about an eye problem and a cold.

In late April 1931, he suffered an attack of appendicitis and underwent an appendectomy.

He was always asking friends to pick up the bill, not because he expected them to pay but because his handlers, his father's moneymen, would square accounts later. And they usually did, though occasionally some of his creditors would have to make embarrassing requests for payment of loans or debts that he had overlooked.

Traveling to the Cape in a chauffeur-driven Rolls-Royce, his family rented a two-and-a-half-acre estate overlooking the Hyannis Port harbor. There, he learned to swim and enjoy the outdoor activities that became a constant in the family's life.

He came to his maturity with an almost studied indifference to money. He never carried much, if any, cash. Why would someone so well-off need currency to pay for anything? Everyone knew or should have known that he was good for his debts, be it a restaurant check, a clothing bill, or a hotel tab.

In September 1936, he enrolled at Harvard College, where he produced that year's annual "Freshman Smoker", called by a reviewer "an elaborate entertainment, which included in its cast outstanding personalities of the radio, screen and sports world".

He tried out for the football, golf, and swimming teams and earned a spot on the varsity swimming team.

In July 1937, he sailed to France—bringing his convertible—and spent ten weeks driving through Europe. In June 1938, he sailed overseas with his father and older brother to work at the American embassy in London where his father was Ambassador to the Court of St. James's.

He toured Europe, the Soviet Union, the Balkans, and the Middle East in preparation for his Harvard senior honors thesis. He then went to Czechoslovakia and Germany before returning to London on September 1, 1939—the day Germany invaded Poland. Two days later, he was in the House of Commons for speeches endorsing the United Kingdom's declaration of war on Germany. He was sent as his father's representative to help with arrangements for American survivors of the SS *Athenia*.

As an upperclassman at Harvard, he became a more serious student and developed an interest in political philosophy. In his junior year, he made the Dean's List.

In 1940, he completed his thesis, "Appeasement in Munich", about British participation in the Munich Agreement. The thesis became a bestseller under the title *Why England Slept*.

- thirty-six -

On the day he was born (August 27, 1908), his white-haired grandfather leaped onto his big black stallion and thundered across the Texas Hill Country, reining in at every farm to shout: "A United States Senator was born this morning!"

A poor boy in a remote Texas town isolated from the mainstream of early twentieth-century American life, he grew up without indoor plumbing or electricity and sometimes made do on a bare subsistence diet.

His mother had been a teacher of elocution—the art of public speaking—and had worked for an Austin newspaper as a stringer reporter.

His father was the first man in Johnson City to own an automobile.

In the evening, his mother read to him from books she had read with her father long ago…Browning, Milton, Dickens. He liked it better when she talked about when she was a young girl.

He showed himself to be a gifted child. He learned the alphabet from blocks before he was two; knew the Mother Goose rhymes and poems from Longfellow and Tennyson by the age of three; and could read and "spell almost anything he could hear" by the time he was four.

Yet all was not idyllic in his first years. His primacy as the only child receiving his parents' undivided attention ended when he was two with the birth of his sister and was further challenged in the next six years by the birth of three other siblings. His tension at losing center stage in the household manifested itself at age four when he began running away from home and alarming his parents, who feared he might be lost or injured.

Usually he just ran down the lane to his grandfather's house. He also ran away to the nearby one-room schoolhouse because he wanted to play with the older children. After a while, his mother enrolled him in the school. He like being the center of attention, so the teacher held him on her lap while he read aloud.

His mother was more interested in the genteel than the pioneer side of the family. This concern made her come close to turning her child into what other boys would call a sissy.

When he was about four or five, his father cut his long curly hair. "He's a boy," his father said to his mother. "And you're making a sissy out of him. You've got to cut his curls." His mother refused to cut his curls. Then one Sunday when his mother went off to church, his father got the big scissors and cut off all his curls.

One of his prized possessions was a stereopticon, an early version of the View-Master. He would sit for hours exploring the wider world by holding the black instrument and its slides up to the light.

His grandfather's house was just several hundred yards from his own home, and he frequently visited and listened to his grandfather tell tales of cattle drives and Indian skirmishes.

Though his mother was the greatest source of his security, she was also his greatest sources of insecurity. If she became displeased with him, if he disappointed her, she would refuse to touch him, talk to him, to acknowledge his existence. For days after he quit violin lessons, she walked around the house pretending he was dead. And then to make it worse, he had to watch her being especially warm and nice to his father and sisters.

Night after night he had the same terrifying dream: He would see himself sitting absolutely still in a big, straight chair in the middle of the great, open plains while a stampede of cattle was coming toward him. In the dream, he tried to move but he could not. He cried out again and again for his mother, but no one came.

He was an unhappy boy trapped in a divided home, relentlessly tumbled among the impossible demands of an unyielding mother, love offered and then denied in seeming punishment; contempt for a father who had failed, admiration for a father who was a model for a Texas manhood. He was commanded to be what could not be, forced to become what he was not.

He came from a political family. His father served in the Texas legislature for six terms. He felt the pull of politics at young age.

The greatest influence on his young life was his father. His interest in political doings from an early age was palpable. His father took him to work at the state legislature. Often he would come on the House floor and stand or sit next to his father. Though he was not an official page, he would run errands for his father and other members of the House.

The only thing he liked more than spending time in the legislature with his father was going with him on the campaign trail, driving a Model T Ford from farm to farm, up and down the valley, stopping at every door.

At school he established a reputation as an indifferent student who treated everything as a joke. Despite his mother's strong ties to the Baptist Church, he defied her by joining the Christian Church. But that had to do more with a girl he fancied than with a genuine conversion.

From the time he was fifteen he was more interested in running with his friends, sometimes staying out until three and four in the morning. Despite Prohibition, he and his friends bought or stole booze, got drunk, and drove recklessly. One night, he smashed up his father's car.

In May 1924 he completed the eleventh and final grade of Johnson City High School. Not yet sixteen, he was the youngest member of the class and was believed to be the youngest graduate of the school. He ran away to California. But in the spring and summer of 1924 parental pressure on him to go to college was unrelenting. They insisted that he enroll in the Southwest Texas teachers College at San Marcos, where students from unaccredited high schools, like the one in Johnson City, could take twelfth grade courses needed for admission to college.

He got a job as a kind of gofer for the college president, delivering messages to the faculty in an era when telephones were still not in every office. In this role he displayed the gift for sycophancy that was to prove so valuable for him in later life. He was the star of his debate team.

When he was a college student, his fellow students (who used his nickname to his face: "Hiya, Bull," "Howya doin', Bull?") believed not only that he lied to them—lied to them constantly, lied about big matters and small, lied so incessantly that he was, in a widely used phrase, "the biggest liar on campus"—but also that some psychological element impelled him to lie, made him, in one classmate's words, "a man who just could not tell the truth."

He was popular enough to be named summer editor of the college newspaper and to play a major role in winning the student body presidency for one of his friends.

He took a break from college to work as a teacher. He worked at a poor school in South Texas. Most of his students were Mexican Americans. It made him sad to know that they had hard lives ahead of them. He went back to college the next year. After graduating in 1930, he became a high school teacher. But he never forgot his first students in South Texas.

In one of the many paradoxes that would shape his life, he was not simply an impoverished farm boy who made good, but the offspring of prominent southern families. Although he suffered painful self-doubts throughout his life, his heritage was a constant source of belief in his a birthright to govern and lead.

The rural small towns in which he received his elementary, secondary, and college schooling did little to broaden his horizons. Yet he came to maturity believing he was special—a young man destined for exceptional things. And he was. Fueled by his early poverty, his ambition, like Lincoln's, "was a little engine that knew no rest."

- thirty-seven -

He emerged—on January 9, 1913—weighing a formidable eleven pounds, with a strong voice and almost a full head of black hair and dark eyebrows.

The circumstances of his early years were nondescript. He came from humble folk and was born in the turn-of-the-century California equivalent of a log cabin.

His first memory was of falling off a horse-drawn buggy, driven by his mother, when it turned a sharp corner. One of the wheels inflicted a long but shallow cut in the middle of his head, which required extensive stitching. This caused him to brush his hair back straight for the rest of his life, and as a youth it gave him a slightly unfashionable appearance.

He was the second of five sons, two of whom died young. He and his brothers were all named after famous Kings of England. His brothers were outgoing.

His father pursued a living first as an orange- and then a lemon-grove owner and operator. His father had only a sixth-grade education.

His Quaker heritage came from his mother's family. His family attended church on Wednesday nights as well as on Sundays.

His mother was selfless toward others but at home was cold, remote, and undemonstrative, and she devoted most of her attention to her two sickly sons. She was stinting in praise of her brightest son's achievements.

He was a rather self-contained little boy, with a round face and big, dark eyes. He enjoyed good health, despite a bout with pneumonia when he was four.

In his youth, the population of Southern California would grow very quickly, and be recognized as some sort of a laboratory for America.

He was a relatively placid child, serious and studious, and interested in everything. Though not at all effeminate, he liked to play with dolls when he visited families who had little girls.

Life was real and life was earnest in the Quaker community of his childhood, twenty miles from Los Angeles, which was just about to arise as a colossal and garish city that would influence the world.

He went to the little wooden Yorba Linda school, entering grade one in the autumn of 1919, when he was a few months short of his seventh birthday. He sometimes went barefoot, but carried shoes and socks in a paper bag, and always wore a starched white shirt, black bow tie, and knee pants.

He got on well and was such an apt student that he skipped forward to grade three in his second year.

He had a talent for memorizing information. He could recite long passages of text.

He grew up without any really close personal friends.
For many years, the house he grew up in had no running water or electricity. He picked stringbeans on nearby farms.

When he was nine, his family moved to nearby Whittier, which was composed predominantly of transplanted Midwesterners who tended toward conservatism and was dominated by Quakers.

His father opened a gasoline station, later expanding into a grocery store where the entire family worked.

His grandmother had strong feelings about pacifism and very strong feelings about civil liberties.

He listened to the distant train whistles and the roar of the steam engines in the night, and dreamt of the wide world.

He was a precocious child. He had a quick temper.

In high school, he disliked the school bus because of its lack of cleanliness and the body odor many of his fellow students.

In his daily life, he was often fretful. He was socially anxious and could be hopelessly, helplessly awkward.

As a teenager, he often arose at four a.m. to drive to Los Angeles to buy produce for the store.

He was an A student throughout his education, often finishing near the top of his class. He won oratorical contests, had a phenomenal memory, and was valedictorian of his eighth-grade class.

Despite his social awkwardness, he was elected several times to leadership positions by his classmates, indicating an early knack for politics—and high ambitious.

His early life also suggests a propensity for taking risks, putting himself on the line in order to succeed—in school politics, debating, sports.

Despite having a slight build, and no real natural athletic ability, he went out for football. He tried to be "one of the guys," but because of his lack of social skills and his tendency to be a loner, he was more respected than popular in high school.

He was a member of the Latin Club and played Aeneas when they celebrated the two thousandth anniversary of Virgil's birth with a banquet and a production of Aeneas and Dido from the *Aeneid*.

When he graduated from Whittier High School, his parents lacked the means to send him to an elite college. (He had been offered a scholarship to Harvard but his parents couldn't afford the other expenses of sending him there.) He was forced to stay home and attend Whittier College.

He put himself through college.

He tried out for the football team, but was consigned to the bench as a water boy.

In college he led a successful rebellion against the Franklin Club, a group of well-off students who were the powers at the school and had denied him membership; he formed a rival fraternity— the first of his many battles against people of more privilege— and he was elected president of the student body in his senior year.
He acted in several plays in college.

After graduating from college in 1934, he attended Duke University Law School. He held down several jobs while attending Duke on a partial scholarship.

He wasn't happy in his law school years; he was hardworking, serious, and remote (he never had a date in those three years), and he acquired the nickname "Gloomy Gus," though he did get elected to the presidency of the law school bar association for his senior year. A classmate said he was elected out of "genuine respect for his scholarship" rather than because he was better liked than the other candidate.

No great opportunity awaited him after his 1937 graduation. He sought positions at prestigious New York law firms, but received no offers. He applied to be an agent at the Federal Bureau of Investigation, but received no reply.

- thirty-eight -

Tracing the childhood of our thirty-eighth president is a detective story as well as a retelling of familiar truths.

His story is a powerful testament to the way nature and nurture—and in some ways nature giving way to nurture—come together to form who we are.

He was born on July 14, 1913, in Omaha, Nebraska. When he came into to the world, he was named Leslie Lynch King, Jr.

His biological father began abusing his mother while they were on their honeymoon train trip. His mother was able to escape the marriage and get a divorce.

When he was two years old, his mother married a new man. Her new husband loved her son as if he were his own.

He was soon renamed after his stepfather.

They lived in a rented two-family house, and he attended kindergarten a block away.

A study of his early years provides insights into how the values of good character are created and reinforced by networks of family, friends, and community institutions.

At night, he would climb into bed with the latest Horatio Alger book. For poetry, he chose the homespun truisms of Edgar Guest, published regularly in the *Detroit Free Press*.

Even at five years old, he played football and softball. He often came home with a dirty face, torn clothes and skinned knees and elbows.

His mother was a strict parent. Depending on the situation, she reasoned with him by twisting his ear or sending him to his room. She realized her son had her first husband's hot temper.

His family had three rules: Tell the truth; work hard; and come home to dinner on time.

At some point in his childhood, his mother mentioned in an offhand way that she had been married before, and that he had been born before she met his stepfather.

He wept—not in sorrow, but in anger that his real father cared so little. He drifted into sleep repeating his mother's favorite prayer from Proverbs: "Trust in the Lord with all thine heart; and lean not unto thine own understanding. In all thy ways acknowledge Him; and He shall direct thy paths."

His mother and stepfather provided the secure support that fostered a confident young man. His stepfather was a paint salesman. He admired the way his adoptive father plodded tirelessly through every detail of his business.

The time of his boyhood coincided with the rise of sports in American males.

To follow his schoolboy careers is to sense the power of community involvement in a distant mirror—innocent and idealistic compared to its later developments.

He had his own peculiar method of writing. When he was sitting down, he wrote with his left hand. When he was standing up, he wrote with his right hand. His parents and teachers tried to get him to write only with his right hand. But when he was about ten years old, his parents and teachers finally gave up trying to change his writing habits. They let him use both hands to write.

During these years, he also had a problem with stuttering. When he was about ten, the stuttering stopped.

His stepfather took him fishing, and also taught him the importance of hard work and honesty. His mother taught her son to treat people fairly and do the right thing.

On his twelfth birthday he joined the Boy Scouts—a significant rite of passage for him. The Boy Scouts, South High School, and an uneven gridiron, where a young athlete proved his toughness and prowess, provided a setting where a powerful personality could begin to assert itself.

As it came time for him to go to high school, the family weighed the choices. Since they lived on a block where district lines met, he could go to Central High, attended by the upper-middle class; Ottawa Hills, a newer school in an elite neighborhood; or South High, which brought together Italians, Greeks, Poles, Lithuanians, blacks, and recent immigrants from Eastern Europe.

He appeared to be a superior type of young man—husky build, blond good looks, outstanding athletic record. His prowess in football won him a part-time job at a Greek diner across the street from South High.

At summer camp he was assigned to be a swimming coach and assistant counselor—his first experience as a leader. Not only did he like being in charge, but he did so well at instructing younger Scouts and earning merit badges that he was chosen to be one of eight Eagle Scouts appointed by Michigan Governor Fred Green to guide visitors at Fort Mackinac during the summer of 1929. He enjoyed meeting the public. He discovered he could speak and hold an audience's attention.

He was an uncomplicated teenager: a straight-arrow Eagle Scout and football star more interested in cars than girls.

His mother clipped and saved every line printed in the newspaper about her star player.

In the classroom he responded well to South High's good teachers and began to think about his future. He set his ambition: to go to college and become a lawyer.

Diligent in his studies, he also learned by observing his peers, forming an optimistic and lasting personal philosophy: Look for the good in every person—he told a classmate—that way, you will never hate anybody.

He had been brought up right, by committed parents who knew what they were about.

He was named All-City Center for three consecutive years and was chosen in his senior year for the All-State Team in 1931.

He wondered why his (biological) father had waited so many years to find him. Was it because he wanted to brag about a son who was football star? He wanted to ask how his father could boast of buying a new Lincoln, yet had paid nothing for his support or education. He looked at his (biological) father, searching for a resemblance, but found none.

He finished in the top 5 percent of his class and was named the most popular senior by his classmates. As a teenager, he worked at a local restaurant and took up the game of football. Playing center, he became one of the best in the state; his football talent helped him win admission to the University of Michigan.

College was out of the question without outside help, but his high school awarded him a $100 per year athletic scholarship (equivalent to a year's tuition) to attend the University of Michigan. While studying liberal arts in Ann Arbor, he augmented his scholarship by working at a hospital and, every two or three months, by selling his blood.

Both the Detroit Lions and the Green Bay Packers of the National Football League offered him a contract (the professional football draft would not be instituted until the following year).

He assessed the situation as dispassionately and practically as he would any other decisions of his career and decided that "pro football probably wouldn't head anywhere." Instead, in the fall of 1935 he accepted a position at Yale University. For three years he worked as an assistant line coach for the varsity team, head coach for the varsity team, and, despite having never boxed, as head coach of the boxing team—for a yearly salary of $2,400. He was allowed to register part-time for a few law courses on a trial basis. In 1939 he secured the school's permission to attend classes full-time, and he got his law degree in 1941, graduating in the top third of his class.

He enlisted in the navy in April 1942, and because he had a college degree, he was commissioned an ensign. In December 1945 he was discharged as a lieutenant with ten battle stars.

- thirty-nine -

He was born in Plains, Georgia, on October 1, 1924. At birth he was endowed with the best traits of both sides of his family.

Because his mother was a nurse, she delivered him at the hospital in Plains, making him the first American President born in a hospital.

He grew up with two younger sisters. He also had a baby brother.

While growing up on his family's farm, he and his brothers and sisters had lots of chores to do. His family grew peanuts, watermelons, sugar cane, and cotton.

He looked up to his father as a hero. His father employed about two hundred sharecroppers who worked on his farm and traded some of their crops for rent.

The Great Depression, which began around the same time he entered grade school, devastated Plains. His family had more luck than most. His father was forced to shut his grocery store, but because he lacked debt and had accumulated a sufficient amount of cash, he was able to take advantage of depressed prices and purchase more land as well as a local insurance and mortgage company.

Although his family's home wasn't big and fancy, his family was better off than most. His house had no running water or bathrooms inside. He drew water from the well in the yard and hauled it to the house for cooking, laundry, and washing up.

Very few farm homes had a telephone, but there was one in his family's house.

When he was six years old, he set his first goal. He wanted to join the navy and be a sailor like his Uncle Gordy who wore an impressive officer's uniform and sent postcards from exotic places where he served.

Growing up he had a tree house, a tire swing, a pony, and bicycles.

His father loved to play tennis and built a tennis court near their house. His father also dug a small swimming pool behind their house.

He was a studious child who avoided trouble. He helped his parents on the farm, tackling everything from chopping wood to picking cotton. One of his favorite things to do outdoors was to sit with his father in the evenings, listening to boxing matches, baseball games, and political conventions on a battery operated radio; there was no electricity in their home before the late 1930s.

He learned to help others at a young age from the influence of his parents.

At times he dreamed of what it might be like to live in distant foreign lands. He read lots of adventure books.

His mother encouraged a love of books. When his mother wanted him to do a chore for her, she asked first what he was doing. If he said he was reading, she excused him from the task.

He learned to accept most jobs he was given and usually didn't complain at all. His least favorite job was applying a mixture of arsenic, molasses, and water to cotton buds. The poisonous, gooey mixture would coat his pants and attract thousands of flies. By the end of the day, the sticky mess dried so hard that he could stand his pants up in the corner of his room.

As a young boy, he began to form lifelong feelings about religion. His family belonged to the Baptist Church.

Early on he formed opinions about segregation and racial injustice, too. He always hated the idea of segregation. Most of his neighbors were African Americans, sharecroppers who rented homes and land from farmers like his father.

His father was a generous-spirited, larger-than-life figure who was well liked by everyone—blacks as well as whites—despite his strongly held segregationist views.

As a boy, he delighted in how the red clay dirt felt on his bare feet. He didn't routinely begin wearing shoes until about the age of thirteen, when etiquette dictated that he put on shoes for church and school.

He loved the land just as his daddy did.

He worked as hard as his parents did. One of his first jobs was to sell boiled peanuts. He took his wagon into the fields and filled it with peanut vines, and pulled it home again. He picked off the peanuts, washed the dirt from them, and soaked them overnight in salty water. He boiled the peanuts for thirty minutes, let them dry, and then put the peanuts into small paper sacks.

His father called him "hotshot."

He launched other successful moneymaking ventures as well. At various times he partnered with his cousin to sell hamburgers and hot dogs on Main Street (a nickel each), ice cream outside the bank (three scoops for a nickel), old newspaper to a fish market for wrapping fish, and scrap iron for salvage (twenty cents per hundred pounds).

When he was eleven, his father installed a windmill to provide running water for the kitchen and bathroom.

While in high school, he did all he could to prepare for the Naval Academy admission exam. In his senior year, he worried that his five-foot-three-inch height and one-hundred-twenty-one pound weight would keep him out. He gave up his part-time job so he could rest more, on the theory that rest would make him grow. He also stuffed himself with bananas hoping they would fatten him up. He walked on Coca-Cola bottles to raise his arches so that he would not be turned down for flat feet, and he worried that his grades would not be good enough.

When he graduated from high school, his parents agreed it would be a good idea for him to attend the U.S. Naval Academy in Annapolis, Maryland.

He would prove to have a keen business mind as well as a growing instinct for fairness. Peanuts were to remain the primary source of his income for the bulk of the next forty-eight years.

- forty -

His father was a drunk.
His mother was a saint.

Tampico, Illinois, the place where he was born (on February 6, 1911), had a population of only 820. In the days after his birth, his father often referred to him as the "fat little Dutchman." Soon, family and friends were referring to him as "Dutch." This nickname stuck, and people called him Dutch for the rest of his life.

His family moved numerous times before he turned six.

Although he always had lots of playmates, during his first years he was a little introverted and slow to make really close friends. He liked to draw cartoons and caricatures, and for a while fancied himself earning a living as an artist.

In hand-me-down overalls, he hiked the hills on the south side of the Rock River, tried (unsuccessfully) to trap muskrats at the river's edge, and played "Cowboys and Indians" on hillsides above the river. As a special hobby, he collected birds' eggs. He was always climbing trees to get them.

Though his family was poor, he never knew it. He had an upbeat outlook on life from the very beginning.

He and his brother always called their mother and father by their first names.

Before he entered school, his mother took the time to sit down every night and read books to him and his brother, following each word with her finger while her sons watched over her shoulder. Before the age of five, he suddenly realized he could read. As he grew older, he excitedly borrowed adventure and sports books from the library.

Two things made it hard for him to make friends at his new school: he was shy and far ahead of his classmates with his reading.

Even as a child, he had an unusual appetite for books.

He read about the Great War in Europe in the newspaper, but he much preferred to read *The Boys' Annual* and adventure stories about people lost in Alaska or even about outer space. He wanted to learn all he could about the world, which was a challenge for a five year old living in the western Illinois town of Galesburg.

He enjoyed reading self-improvement novels by writers such as Harold Bell Wright and Horatio Alger. He later attributed his embrace of Christianity and his sunny outlook on the lessons he learned from reading Wright's *That Printer of Udell's* (1903), which tells of small-town boy whose drunken father leaves his family to starve.

He took comfort in knowing that he was not the only kid at school who put cardboard inside the bottom of his boots when the soles wore through or wore his older brother's hand-me-downs.

What he enjoyed most was watching the Saturday movie matinees at the local opera house. A different Western feature played nearly every Saturday afternoon, and he carried coal for the boilers at the opera house in exchange for free admission to the movie. As far as he was concerned, it was the best deal he ever made. He always sat in the front row, his imagination fired up by the Westerns and the pounding opera house piano, which provided the musical soundtrack for the silent movie.

His father was a shoe salesman. His father had a difficult time keeping a job, but his mother always took care of the family's needs.

When his mother thought that he and his brother were old enough to know, she sat her sons down and explained why their father sometimes disappeared and told them the reason for those sudden unexpected trips from home. His mother said their father had a sickness that he couldn't control—an addiction to alcohol.

On the eve of the Fourth of July when he was eleven, he managed to obtain some prohibited fireworks, including a particularly powerful variety known as a torpedo. As he approached the town bridge that spanned the Rock River, he let a torpedo fly against a brick wall beside the bridge. The ensuing blast was appropriately loud, but as he savored it, a car pulled up and driver ordered him to get inside. He'd been taught not to get into automobiles with strangers, and refused. When the man flashed a police badge, he got inside. At the police station, he was taken to see the police chief, who he knew spent a lot of time playing pinochle with his father. His father had to pay a fine of $14.50, which was big money in those days.

One cold, blustery, winter's night as he came home from the YMCA, he nearly stumbled over a lump near the front door. It was his father, lying in the snow, his arms outstretched, flat on his back. He leaned over to see what was wrong, and he smelled whiskey on his father's breath. His father had found his way home from a speakeasy and had passed out. For a moment or two, he looked down at his father and thought about continuing into the house and going to bed. But he couldn't do it. He tried to wake his father but couldn't. He grabbed a piece of his father's overcoat and dragged him into the house.

When he was thirteen or fourteen, his father took the family for a Sunday drive through the green countryside. His mother had left her eyeglasses in the back seat, and he picked up her glasses and put them on. The next instant, he let out a yelp. He'd discovered a world he didn't know existed before. By picking up his mother's glasses, he discovered that he was extremely nearsighted.

With new glasses to correct his nearsightedness, he soon gazed with even greater excitement at the Friday night cliffhangers and Westerns at the local movie theater.

He loved sports; he tried out for football in high school and loved just about every other sport there was. Unfortunately, he was small for his age, and he sat on the bench most of the season. The following summer, he found a job working for a local construction company. The physical work helped him develop strong muscles.

The earnings from his employment went to aiding the family's finances, with some set aside for this own education.

He started taking swimming lessons and became an excellent swimmer. Over the next few years, as he continued to swim and stay physically active, he grew even stronger. He also grew tall.

While working as a lifeguard, he once rescued an elderly man's false teeth. Many times, he spotted swimmers struggling in the river. Plunging into the current, he would swim out and pull them to safety. He was proud to have saved as many as seventy-seven swimmers!

He suddenly found himself the center of attention. He loved the attention he got, especially from the local girls. With each passing summer he grew stronger, more handsome, and more confident. He was the perfect specimen of an athlete, tall, willowy, muscular, brown, good looking. Of course, the girls were always flocking around him. Not only did learning come easily to him, but the other students liked his friendly, positive personality. Only his father's tragic alcoholism ruined his complete joy in growing up.

As a teenager he really loved acting. He started performing in plays and found that he loved being onstage. He played parts in school plays whenever he got the chance. By the time he graduated, he had played the lead role in several plays.

He craved approval and applause, thanks to growing up the son of an alcoholic father who gave him little of either.

College in those days was the reserve of the few; neither of his parents had attended college. Room, board, and tuition at Eureka College would use up his four hundred dollars in savings in just one year. Impressed by his enthusiasm, however, the dean of students granted him an athletic scholarship to cover half of his tuition. To scrape together the rest of the money, he took on a number of campus jobs. At his fraternity (Tau Kappa Epsilon), he rolled up his sleeves and washed dishes after meals. At a girls' dormitory, he waited on tables. He also sometimes helped the college groundskeepers rake leaves and shovel snow from the sidewalks. In the classroom he majored in sociology and economics.

In his freshman year, he was one of the leaders of a student boycott that came when the president of the chronically cash-strapped college proposed cancelling courses and laying off faculty to save money. The students suggested that he serve as the voice of students, when their concerns were presented to the trustees and administration.

In the summer of 1933, he'd been able work a seventh summer as a lifeguard at Lowell Park and had saved enough money to finance a job-hunting trip. He had a new college diploma that summer and a lot of dreams. He made up his mind to follow his dream. He knew it was almost impossible to just go to Hollywood and become a movie star. So he tried the next best thing, which was to become a radio sports announcer.

He became well known as a baseball radio announcer. Then, while on a trip to California, a friend arranged a screen test (a film audition) for him. A few days after returning to Iowa, he received a seven-year contract from Warner Brothers Studio— starting at $200 per week—to act in movies!

- forty-one -

He was born in Milton, Massachusetts on June 12, 1924.

He was named for his grandfather, who was always called "Pop" by his family. So as a young boy, he quickly became known as "Poppy." The nickname stuck through his childhood and into his adult years.

The U.S.A. was plunged into the Great Depression beginning with the 1929-31 financial collapse, but he and his family were totally insulated from this crisis. Before and after the crash, their lives were a frolic, sealed off from the concerns of the population at large.

He learned about friendship from his three brothers and one sister. He and his older brother loved spending time together. They always shared a bedroom, sometimes playing baseball there, batting around their dad's rolled up socks.

He attended Greenwich Country Day School, entering first grade a year early so he could start school with his older brother. The family chauffer drove them to school every morning.

Both of his parents were good athletes and always played to win. He excelled at baseball and soccer and became the captain of both teams. Once, he told his mother that he'd scored three goals in a soccer game. She replied to him, "That's nice, but how did *the team* do?"
His father was strict and formal. His mother was a little like an army drill sergeant.

He was more like his mother. His mother always told him to be a team player, and she taught him not to brag about his talents. Be a good sport and don't complain, she told him, be honest and help others.

Once he used an ax—his mother had told him not to do it. He cut himself on the leg—a deep cut. He lied to her about what happened. But she knew he was lying. She didn't spank him and she got him to admit, on his own, that he had not told the truth, and that he had used the ax when she had told him not to. She explained to him about never lying.

As a boy he was fondly known as "Have Half" for his disposition to share what he had with others.

Older people tended to adore him.

He was an empathetic child, drawing out others. During an informal playground race, he saw a heavy classmate got stuck in an obstacle course barrel and couldn't get out. As the other children pressed on to the finish line, he stopped to pull the boy out. He recalled, "I saw him there and I got to thinking, 'I've never been the guy who wasn't picked for the team or was left waiting in line.' Seeing him stuck made me think about how I'd feel. I'd want somebody to help me. So I helped."

One friend, two years behind him in elementary school, remembers him as the one he looked up to and idolized. Years later, in an ethics course at Yale University, they met and chatted as if no time had gone by.

He and his older brother once paid a neighborhood girl a dime to run naked through the house. When his father found out, he was enraged.

He learned easily and rapidly. His marks at Greenwich Country Day School were always quite satisfactory and he was frequently on the honor roll. He seemed to have taken pride in standing well in his class.

Every noun he touched became a proper noun.

In the summers, he and his family visited his grandfather at his house in Maine. He learned how to fish and handle a lobster boat. While everyone in his family had been musically inclined, he couldn't play the piano or carry a tune.

He went to Phillips Academy in Andover, Massachusetts. Young for his class at thirteen, he struggled at first. Soon, other students were drawn to him; they felt protected and secure in his orbit.

He was the kind of boy who seemed well suited to living life by a code of camouflaged competitiveness. He was not an intellectual or even intellectually curious. He was more of an achiever, a doer.

He was tall and skinny, with a high forehead and wide-set eyes that looked out at the world with a precocious gravity from under soft and delicately curved brows. The rest of his face—the narrow cheeks and the line of his long, slender jaw—was hairless and smooth, saved from prettiness only by a generous, slightly cleft chin and the quick, lopsided aw-heck grin that dismissed his own good looks and made him, so readily, one of the guys.

He was seventeen when he met the girl he would marry at a Christmas dance at the Round Hill Club in Greenwich, Connecticut. He soon invited her to Andover senior prom.

As a senior he nearly died of a staph infection in his right arm. Surviving this ordeal, which required a lengthy stay in the hospital, may have given him a sense of mission if not destiny.

He graduated from Andover and joined the Navy on the June 12, 1942—his eighteenth birthday. Most of his friends waited a year or two, but he wanted to go right away.

He was accepted at Yale but he wanted to become a Navy pilot. He was nervous when he began Navy training. He had to face his fears. For one thing, he was left-handed and controls in the plane were set up for right-handed pilots.

He was the youngest man in flight training school and got teased all the time. He got his Navy wings in Corpus Christi, Texas, in June 1943. At age eighteen, he was the youngest pilot in the Navy at the time.

Just past his twentieth birthday, he looked so young he didn't seem ready to operate a car, much less the biggest bomber aircraft in the Pacific fleet. He was only a year past winning his wings as the youngest flier in the Navy.

He flew Avenger torpedo planes from the flight deck of the *San Jacinto*, saw action off Marcus and Wake Islands, was shot down over Chichi-Jima near the Japanese home islands, and was rescued by an American submarine. Altogether, he flew fifty-eight missions and won the Distinguished Flying Cross, the Navy's second highest combat decoration.

He was discharged September 18, 1945, and entered Yale as a freshman with the class of returning servicemen. He was one among eight hundred veterans at Yale on the G.I. Bill. Majoring in economics and sociology, he finished in the top 10 percent of his class and graduated Phi Beta Kappa.

He led Yale to the NCAA College World Series championship games in Kalamazoo, Michigan, in both 1947 and 1948 (they lost to the University of California in 1947 and to USC in 1978). He played first base, and according to the Yale Daily News, was "one of the flashiest fielding first basemen in collegiate circles."

- forty-two -

He was a big, large baby—
he wasn't premature at all.

He was born on August 19, 1946 and grew up amid domestic chaos.

His biological father was dead and his stepfather was an abusive alcoholic.

His mother moved to New Orleans to study nursing soon after he was born. She left him in Hope, Arkansas with her parents, who ran a small grocery store.

He was a talkative, sensitive, chubby little boy.

Like many children in such circumstances, he threw his energy into personal achievement. And he became a natural conciliator—instinctually eager for people to get along and feel good, and instinctually good at getting them to do so.

When he was two, his grandmother began preparing homemade flashcards with letters and numbers on them. She taught him the rudiments of reading while he sat in his high chair. She dressed him in knickers and fine pin-striped outfits. She introduced him to church at age three.

Only his mother and grandmother harbored grand notions of what might be in store for him.

The little boy loved to wear his Hopalong Cassidy outfit with black pants, black coat and hat, and a T-shirt with the cowboy star's picture on it.

He spent two years in a catholic grade school and raised his hand in class so much that one of the nuns gave him a C for being a busy body.

When he was eight, he dressed himself in a suit on Sunday mornings and walked alone the half-mile down Park Avenue to Park Place Baptist Church, carrying his old leather-bound Bible.

He was never hard as a child. He didn't demand things. He always had some amazing abilities.

His grandfather taught him not to judge people by the color of their skin. People always said he seemed more grown-up than other kids his age.

Back when he was a child, at age ten, he watched—entranced— the national Democratic political convention on the family's first television set. He was fascinated to learn how elections and politics worked. Even at such a young age, he understood what was going on.

He would have been valedictorian of his sixth-grade class, except he got a B in deportment for talking.

His mother adored him and was deeply supportive—as were his grandparents—and he was an exceptionally bright and gregarious youngster. He made close friends and nurtured these relationships across the years.

He described himself in junior high as "fat, uncool, and hardly popular with the girls." But he was smart, articulate, and always interested in politics and public life.

He was an excellent student. The only problem his teachers had with him was when he shouted out answers before other kids could even raise their hands.

At night he would hear his parents fighting.

He was inculcated into the Kabuki dance of adultery, jealousy, and lying from an early age, and it became an unconscious paradigm that was burned into his psyche.

He never talked about family secrets with anyone: a friend, a neighbor, a teacher, a pastor, a counselor. And later on he noted that while we all have them, some secrets "can be an awful burden to bear, especially if some sense of shame is attached to make us feel we can't live without them, that we wouldn't be who we are without them."

He was only sixteen, but one of the bigger boys physically at six foot three and two hundred pounds, with a wave of brown hair and a good-natured manner.

He really consumed school. He was an attentive listener who would follow the speaker with his eyes. He acquired knowledge like a magnet gets steel. Yeah, he was an intellect.

He read all the time. He was studying the world. He wasn't in the geek crowd, but he competed academically at a geek level. He always did his homework.

While big for his age and rather clumsy, certainly not a gifted athlete, he did make his mark right through high school as a musician. He loved music: classical, jazz, Elvis Presley. His instrument was saxophone and he was in the high school concert and marching bands as well as a jazz trio. For seven summers, he attended band camp at the University of Arkansas.

He was, at seventeen, during his final year at home, if the not the master of the house at least the central force within it. His bedroom was the largest in the house, the master bedroom really, with its own bath.

His potential for public service was honed in high school, when he attended the Arkansas Boys State civics program and was elected the state representative to the American Legion's Boy Nation in Washington, DC. When the group visited the White House, he asked whether he could have his picture taken with

President Kennedy in the Rose Garden.

His time was taken up with his extracurricular activities because he was into and doing everything. He was very serious about saxophone. He loved jazz—he often had Dave Brubeck on or Stan Getz.

The sense of him around school was that he *was* somebody and would *be* somebody. He was a presence.

Even at a very early age, he decided it was important for him to be a good citizen. He really wanted to make his community and country a better place to live.

He tried to hide his family's problems. He appeared happy to his teachers and friends, and he worked hard not to let other people discover his pain.

He had friends across the color line and, even as a boy, rejected the racist policies of the governor of Arkansas and other home-state politicians. As a teenager, he cried, sitting alone, watching Martin Luther King's famous "I Have a Dream Speech" at the Lincoln Memorial.

He was elected president of the junior class, and was the winner of so many awards that he was kept from running for student council or senior class president only by a school rule restricting students from too many activities.

At Georgetown, he ran and won the election as president of the freshman class. He would be re-elected as sophomore class president. He had a remarkable capacity to meet, make, and keep new friends and to enlist some of them to work for him in his campaigns.

He excelled in debates and political maneuvering. He had enormous energy and seemed to operate on less sleep than almost anyone else.

To help pay for college, he got a job working in the office of Arkansas Senator William Fulbright. He knew what he would do with his life. He would become a politician.

He was such a good student in college that he was offered a Rhodes Scholarship to study at Oxford University in England.

- forty-three -

Born in New Haven, Connecticut, on July 6, 1946, he was the Roman candle of the family, bright, hot, a sparkler--and the likeliest to burn the fingers.

When he turned two, his family moved to Midland, Texas, an everyday, working-class town, next to hot, dusty, Texas oil fields. He came from a pretty wealthy family. His father was part owner of a successful oil company. He had all of his old man's high spirits, but none of his taste for accommodation.

His father noticed that—as a three-year-old—he tried to say everything he heard and the results were often hilarious. He seemed to be very happy wherever he was, and he was very good about amusing himself.

Friends and relatives remember him as being an extremely active child. He passed his days swimming in the pool, riding bikes, climbing behind the bleachers at Friday night football games, playing catcher on his Little League baseball team, and attending family barbecues. He loved playing baseball more than anything. He had one of the best baseball card collections around. His idol was Willie Mays, a New York Giants Superstar.

He attended the Sam Houston Elementary School. He was the class clown, always cracking jokes and wanting to be the center of attention. Nobody blinked when he tossed a football through his West Texas elementary school window. His little league coach never said a word about the lousy-hitting kid.

He probably could have gotten better grades. Instead of doing his homework, he spent too much time memorizing the names and positions of major-league ball players.

He had a very happy childhood. There was one event, though, that caused him and his parents the greatest sadness of all. When he was only seven, his four-year-old sister died of a blood disease called leukemia.

He discovered how serious his sister's illness was while at school one day. His parents, who had been in New York with his sister Robin while she received treatment, drove to pick him up two days after his sister had died of cancer. He was wheeling a record player to the principal's office when he saw his parents' car. He ran to a teacher to tell her that he had to go because his parents and sister were waiting for him. "I run over to the car," he recalled," and there's no Robin."

In addition to the pain of losing Robin, he was upset that his parents had not told him how sick she had been. They said they did not want to burden him because there was nothing he could do.

One time he attended a football game with his father and some of his friends. When his vision was blocked by adults, he turned to his father and said he wished he were dead like his sister Robin up in heaven. After a brief silence, his father asked him why. "I bet she can see the game better up there than we can here," he said.

When he saw how sad his parents were, though, he started to do whatever he could to cheer them up. He became kind of a clown at home. He also became a jokester at school. He once painted Elvis Presley-like type sideburns on his face to get a laugh. He used his excellent sense of humor to attract friends all through school.

His family attended the First Presbyterian Church in Midland.

He went to an exclusive preparatory school in Massachusetts. At Phillips Academy in Andover, he was the head cheerleader and people fed off his energy, the way he was always just there, always remembering people's names, birthdays, habits, parents, brothers, sisters.

He did OK in school and in sports, but he was remembered more for the great parties he threw. He was a genius at making friends and having fun.

Although he never made the honor roll, he was popular on campus. He made friends easily and earned the nickname Lip because he had an opinion on just about everything and often spoke sharply.

He was also the member of a rock-and-roll band, the Torqueys. He didn't play an instrument. His job was to stand onstage and sing.

He memorized everyone's name the instant he met them, and it pleased them that he did. It was something he did even better than his father and grandfather. Ten, twenty, hundreds of names, he could recite them all, total recall, minutes after meeting them. And everyone, even if it took him a while to figure it out, got a nickname.

For college, he attended Yale University in Connecticut, the same college his father and grandfather attended.

It did not appear that he had the grades to get into such a distinguished school as Yale. Because he was the relative of prominent Yale graduates, he was admitted to the university to keep the family tradition, or legacy, alive.

He did not enjoy being away from home. And he didn't really like living on the East Coast. But he wanted to follow in his father's footsteps and go to Yale.

As a freshman, he was a pitcher on the Yale baseball team. Two years later, he began to play rugby, a game that is a lot like football.

He decided he did not like many of the people at Yale. He felt they often pretended that they were better than everybody else. He also thought they were too proud of going to school like Yale. He did not like to act like he was better than anybody. He often wore wrinkled clothes and drove an old, beat-up car.

He was a weak student who feared flunking out and who graduated near the bottom of his class.

When he decided to become a pledge for Delta Kappa Epsilon, he joined fifty other young men in hoping to be accepted into the fraternity. At one point, the older members tried to embarrass him and the other pledges by challenging them to name all fifty pledges. Most of the initiates could only remember five or six names, but when it was his turn, he was able to recite the name of every single pledge.

After graduating from Yale, he joined the Texas National Guard.

He went to, earned a college degree from Yale, and completed a master's in business administration from Harvard.

- forty-four -

On August 4, 1961, a baby boy was born at Kapi'olani Medical Center in Honolulu.

He weighed eight pounds, two ounces. The name he was given was the same as his father's. His first name means "blessed" in Swahili, an African language.

His father was from Kenya, a country in Africa. His mother was born in Wichita, Kansas.

Shortly after his birth, his parents split up. During his first years, he didn't wonder why his father was missing.

His mother was white, but he could not ignore the fact that he was black, even when he didn't feel like a member of that community. He looked black. His mother told him that he got his eyebrows from her, but his wit and character from his father, as did so many of his other features: his nose; his cheeks and smile; his hair texture; his long, lean body; the ginger color of his skin, which was like a swirl of milk in coffee.

In 1967, he and his mother moved to Indonesia to live with his new stepfather. He played in rice patties and rode water buffalo. He also made friends with other children. In the backyard he found a pond with a real baby crocodile. He spent his days catching crickets and flying kites.

These were years he would later remember as "a joyous time, full of adventure and mystery."

During his time in Indonesia, he lived in the country's capitol, Jakarta. The first house he lived in did not have a flush toilet, and the streets in the neighborhood were not yet paved. While there, his stepfather gave him a pet ape named Tata. He also tried cool new foods such as snake meat and roasted grasshopper!

He began his education at an Indonesian grammar school. One classmate remembered him for his ambition, "At the time here in Indonesia, all the parents pushed their kids: 'You have to become a doctor' or 'You have to become an engineer.' But he wrote that he'd like to be president."

Learning self-defense was only one of his activities. He studied Indonesia's languages and customs.

His mother told him that he had a wonderful father—fiercely intelligent, with a deep baritone voice and a way of commanding people's attention. His mother showed him pictures of his father. She told him that his father loved him very much.

He was beginning to doubt the stories he had been told by his mother about his father's greatness. He barely knew his father and only saw him once (for a period of one month) in 1971.

He was impressed by the way his father could catch the attention of everyone in a room simply by walking in, speaking in his confident manner, moving gracefully.

His father brought him some wooden carvings. He danced with his father to African music. His father believed the boy had been watching too much TV and not studying enough.

His mother was concerned that he was not receiving a proper education (in Indonesia). She thought he would be better off if he went to school back in America, so she sent him to her parents in the summer of 1971.

Family pictures show him happily riding his tricycle or perched on a fence with his mother's arm around him. In another picture from those days, he frolics in the surf with his grandfather.

His grandfather was a furniture salesman, while his grandmother worked for a bank.

Now that he was in Hawaii again, his grandparents enrolled him in the Punahou School. He stayed at that school for eight years.

On his first day he was asked if his father in Kenya was a cannibal. "Certainly not," he said. He coolly explained that his father was actually a prince.

He spent his days playing outside, often accompanying his grandfather to the beach or park. He went spearfishing with his Gramps. And wherever he went, he saw many people of all different colors. He ate rice candy and roast pork and a Hawaiian food called poi.

He knew that sometimes people treated him differently because of his skin color. He stood out as one of the few African-Americans enrolled in the school. A girl at school wanted to touch his wiry hair.

As a young kid, he didn't notice that he was half black and half white. But as he grew older, he started to see that he was half black living mostly among white people.

When he looked into the mirror, he saw a young black man. But he didn't know how to be black. And no one was there to teach him.

He lived for nearly ten years with his grandparents, but he started to feel like he didn't belong. As he got older, he started to act out. Though he was an honors student and an athlete, he also liked to go to parties.

He called his grandmother Toot, after the Hawaiian word "Tutu" meaning grandmother. His mother and grandparents talked to him about his father, but they never criticized his father.

He did very well in both school and sports. He was also editor of the school magazine and a member of the school's choir. His other interests included jazz, fishing, and surfing. His school's basketball team even won the state championship in 1979!

He once came across an article about a black man who had tried to whiten his skin with chemicals. It made no sense to him. In many ways, his race was still a puzzle he was struggling to understand.

He was still trying to figure out exactly who he was. He looked like a black student, complete with an afro hairdo. But living with his white grandparents and knowing two sides of his heritage made it difficult to settle on an identity.

He cherished his full afro and could spend a long time picking at it in order to make it appear just right.

As he became a teenager, home was an unremarkable apartment building in Honolulu, which could easily be mistaken for some nondescript medical office building that houses a handful of doctors.

On long walks, he kept looking at people. He hoped to find where he fit in.

He listened to his mother's stories and imagined the father he did not know. All he had of his father were imprints he had left behind with others: images on photographic paper and memories burned inside the minds of those who had known him. Could he believe in a man he remembered seeing only once?

By the time of his high school graduation, he was aware of how alone he was, being black and not black at the same time. He couldn't shake the feeling that he was on the outside looking in, and he wasn't sure how to deal with it.

He graduated without mishap, was accepted into several respectable schools, and settled on Occidental College in Los Angeles mainly because he'd met a girl from Brentwood while she was vacationing in Hawaii with her family.

He knew just one of his parents and, as much as his mother tried, she couldn't give him all the knowledge he needed to become a man. There were other male figures in his life—his grandfather, his stepfather, an older black poet—but which of them was he supposed to emulate?

- forty-five -

He was the fourth of five children in his family, born on June 14, 1946.

His father, with his thick moustache and hair combed back, was a stern, formal man who insisted on wearing a tie and jacket at home. A conservative Republican who admired Barry Goldwater, his father forbade his children from cursing or calling each other by nicknames.

His mother, a Scottish immigrant, relished attention, thrusting herself to the center of every social gathering. Fair, tall, and slender with blue eyes and blond hair, his mother spoke with a hint of a brogue.

When he was three he went to the Carousel Pre-School, a new nursery program in Jamaica Estates, Queens. He was a beautiful little boy, very blond and buttery. He was a nice size for his age, very attractive, social, and outgoing. He wasn't fat, but he was sturdy, and really quite jolly.

For kindergarten, he went to the private Kew-Forest School, which required skirts for girls and ties and blazers for boys. His father was a board member of the school.

He has said that he hasn't changed since the first grade.

During dodgeball games, he was known for jumping and pulling his knees up to avoid balls thrown at him.

His father's success as a real estate developer paid for the private schools, limousines, and a 23-room house to which he and his four siblings grew accustomed. His father wasn't shy about flashing symbols of wealth either. Unlike most families in the neighborhood, his had a cook, a chauffeur, and an intercom system.

He recalls that his mother had been fascinated by the coronation of Queen Elizabeth II, in 1953. As a boy he had been impressed by his mother's interest as she eagerly watched every minute of the live TV broadcast of the event.

Even in elementary school, he was a very assertive, aggressive kid. In the second grade, he actually gave a teacher a black eye—he punched his music teacher because he didn't think he knew anything about music and he almost got expelled.

He had the most amazing train set. He had all these special gadgets and gates and switches.

He impressed classmates with his athleticism, shenanigans, and refusal to acknowledge mistakes, even one so trivial as misidentifying a popular professional wrestler. No matter his pals' ridicule, he doubled down, insisting wrestler Antonio Rocca's name was "Rocky Antonino."

His face crowned by a striking blond pompadour, he commanded attention with playground taunts, classroom disruptions, and distinctive countenance, even then his lips pursed in a way that would inspire future mimics.

He had a reputation for saying anything that came into his head. Taller than his classmates, he exuded an easy confidence and independence.

His best sport was baseball. By sixth grade, his power as a right-handed hitter was enough that fielders shifted to left field when he batted. If he had hit the ball to right, he could've had a home run because no one was there. But he always wanted to hit the ball through people. He wanted to overpower them.

A fierce competitor, he would erupt in anger, smashing a baseball bat, if he made an out.

In school he misbehaved so often that his initials became his friends' shorthand for detention.

His father instilled thrift in him by coaxing him to redeem soda-bottle deposits and forcing him to get summer jobs and paper routes. When it rained, he delivered newspapers from the back of a chauffeured limousine.

By junior high, inspired by the battles between the Sharks and the Jets in *West Side Story*, he was sneaking onto the subway and amassing a collection of switchblades, according to friends.

When he was thirteen, his father abruptly sent him to a military boarding school, where instructors struck him if he misbehaved and the requirements included daily inspections and strict curfews.

He was essentially banished from the family home. He hadn't known anything but living with his family in a luxurious setting, and all of a sudden he was sent away.

At New York Military Academy, he wore a crew cut, a thick wool uniform and was awoken daily by a recording of reveille.

At the beginning, he didn't like the idea of being told what to do—like make your bed, shine your shoes, brush your teeth, clean the sink, do your homework. He did his best to fit in, once even refusing to let his parents visit unless they left the chauffeur at home.

Instead of steaks prepared by his family's cook, he sat in a crowded mess hall and filled his plate from vats of meatloaf, spaghetti, and something called "mystery mountains," a stew of deep-fried leftovers remade as meatballs. Instead of his own bathroom, he had to shower with fellow cadets. Instead of his father, his new taskmaster was a no-nonsense combat veteran who had served in World War II who had seen Mussolini's dead body hanging from a rope.

At the military academy, he grew taller, more muscular and tougher.

He was headstrong and determined. He would sit with his arms folded with this look on his face—surly—almost daring someone to say one thing or another that wouldn't settle with him.

Struck with a broomstick during a fight, he tried to push a fellow cadet out a second-floor window, only to be thwarted when two other students intervened.

If nothing else, the military academy taught him a lesson that would prove valuable in adulthood as he navigated two divorces, bankruptcy and regular spasms of bad publicity: No matter the crisis, he could prevail.

He won medals for neatness and took pride in his grades. He distinguished himself on both the baseball and football teams. He wanted to be number one. He wanted to be noticed. He wanted to be recognized. And he liked compliments.

At last he was in a place where winning really mattered, and he poured himself into doing better than everyone else at everything. In the classroom he could compete for grades and actually managed to get the highest grades in geometry. And on the athletic field he could compete in every sport and be a star.

His ball-field experiences were formative because they made him locally famous and because they instilled in him the habit of winning. By his own estimate he was definitely "the best baseball player in New York," and he would have turned pro except that "there was no real money in it."

To his classmates, he was a blend of friendly and cocky. He boasted that his father's wealth doubled every time he completed a real estate deal. He was self-confident and very soft-spoken, as if he knew he was just passing time until he went on to something greater.

Peers say there were no signs that he treated anyone differently. He met students from all over the U.S., guys from Central and

South America. He got along with everybody.

Nonetheless he never had truly close friends. He wasn't that tight with anyone, his first year roommate recalled.

At the Academy, he learned a lot about discipline, and about channeling his aggression into achievement. In his senior year he was appointed a captain of the cadets.

During spring break senior year, he went on a chaperoned trip to Bermuda with other cadets, and they all rode around on rented motor scooters and met socially appropriate girls on chaperoned trips from their own prep schools.

"Ladies Man" read the caption beneath a photo of him in the senior yearbook.

He began attending Fordham University in the Bronx, mostly because he wanted to be close to home. He got along very well with the Jesuits who ran the school, but after two years, he decided that as long as he had to be in college, he might as well test himself against the best. He applied to the Wharton School of Finance at the University of Pennsylvania and he got in.

While in college from 1964 to 1968, he obtained four student deferments from the draft for the Vietnam War. In late November 1966 he was briefly classified as 1-A, Available for Service. But within a few weeks he was once again reclassified with a 2-S, Student Deferment. He received one more deferment in January 1968, months before he graduated.

His Selective Service records indicate that he was again reclassified as 1-A. But despite having gained a reputation as a physically superior specimen who had excelled in athletics throughout his life, he was suddenly reclassified on October 15, 1968 as 1-Y (which would later be changed to a 4-F, unable to serve). It turned out he had what were classified as bone spurs on the heels of both feet.

After graduating from Wharton in 1968, he joined the family real estate business. He was immediately immersed into the day-to-day management of his father's mini empire, which, after many years, had continued to focus on middle class rental housing in his long held territories of Brooklyn, Queens, and Staten Island.

He eased into the working environment, but within a year was already growing restless at his father's extremely conservative philosophy that, while continuing to be successful, ultimately resulted in a limited vision and, predictably, smaller profit margins.

—U.S. Presidents—

1	George Washington	1789-1797
2	John Adams	1797-1801
3	Thomas Jefferson	1801-1809
4	James Madison	1809-1817
5	James Monroe	1817-1825
6	John Quincy Adams	1825-1829
7	Andrew Jackson	1829-1837
8	Martin Van Buren	1837-1841
9	William Henry Harrison	1841
10	John Tyler	1841-1845
11	James K. Polk	1845-1849
12	Zachary Taylor	1849-1850
13	Millard Fillmore	1850-1853
14	Franklin Pierce	1853-1857
15	James Buchanan	1857-1861
16	Abraham Lincoln	1861-1865
17	Andrew Johnson	1865-1869
18	Ulysses S. Grant	1869-1877
19	Rutherford B. Hayes	1877-1881
20	James A. Garfield	1881
21	Chester A. Arthur	1881-1885
22	Grover Cleveland	1885-1889
23	Benjamin Harrison	1889-1893
24	Grover Cleveland	1893-1897
25	William McKinley	1897-1901
26	Theodore Roosevelt	1901-1909
27	William H. Taft	1909-1913
28	Woodrow Wilson	1913-1921
29	Warren G. Harding	1921-1923

30	Calvin Coolidge	1923-1929
31	Herbert Hoover	1929-1933
32	Franklin D. Roosevelt	1933-1945
33	Harry S. Truman	1945-1953
34	Dwight D. Eisenhower	1953-1961
35	John F. Kennedy	1961-1963
36	Lyndon B. Johnson	1963-1969
37	Richard M. Nixon	1969-1974
38	Gerald R. Ford	1974-1977
39	Jimmy Carter	1977-1981
40	Ronald Reagan	1981-1989
41	George H. W. Bush	1989-1993
42	Bill Clinton	1993-2001
43	George W. Bush	2001-2009
44	Barack Obama	2009-2017
45	Donald J. Trump	2017-

—BIBLIOGRAPHY—

Adams, John Quincy. *The Lives of James Madison and James Monroe.*
   Phillips, Sampson & Co., 1850.

Adkins, Jan. *John Adams: Young Revolutionary.* Simon & Schuster, 2002.

Alger, Horatio. *From Canal Boy to President.* American Publishers
   Corporation, 1881.

Allen, Walter. *Ulysses S. Grant.* The Riverside Press, 1901

Allison, Andrew M. *The Real Thomas Jefferson.* National Center for
   Constitutional Studies, 1983.

Altman, Alex. "Tribal Warrior". *TIME,* March 14, 2016.

Ambrose, Stephen E. *Eisenhower: Soldier and President.* Simon and
   Schuster, 1990.

Ambrose, Stephen E. *Nixon, Vol.1: The Education of a Politician.* Simon
   and Schuster, 1987.

Ammon, Harry. *James Monroe: The Quest for a National Identity.*
   University of Virginia Press, 1990.

Amoroso, Cynthia. *Presidents of the U.S.A.: Ronald Reagan.* The Child's
   World, 2009.

Anon. *Woodrow Wilson: A Life Worth Reading.* Higher Read LLC, 2014.

Anon. *Franklin D. Roosevelt (FDR).* Shmoop University, 2010.

Arias, Oscar. *American Presidents Series: George Washington for Kids.*
   Children's History Press, 2014.

Author unknown. "Sketch of the Life of Martin Van Buren." *The
   Statesman Supplement,* 1862.

Atler, Jonathan. *The Defining moment: FDR's Hundred Days and the
   Triumph of Hope.* Simon & Schuster, 2006.

Author unknown. *Life of Gen. Franklin Pierce, the Democratic Candidate
   for President.* Morris R. Hamilton, 1852.

Bains, Rae. *James Monroe: Young Patriot.* Troll Associates, 1997.

Balmer, Randall. *Redeemer: The Life of Jimmy Carter.* Basic Books, 2014.

Barnard, Harry. *Rutherford B. Hayes: And His America.* The Bobbs
   Merrill Company, 1954.

Barre, W.L. *The Life and Public Services of Millard Fillmore.* Wanzer,
   McKim & Co., 1856.

Bartlett, D.W. *The Life of Gen. Franklin Pierce, of New Hampshire,
   President of the United States.* Miller, Orton & Mulligan, 1855.

Baker, Jean. *James Buchanan: The American Presidents Series: The 15th
   President.* Macmillan, 2004.

Benge, Janet and Geoff. *John Adams: Independence Forever.* Emerald
   Books, 2012.

Benge, Janet & Geoff. *Ronald Reagan: Destiny at his Side*. Emerald Books, 2010.

Benge, Janet & Geoff. *George Washington: True Patriot*. Emerald Books, 2001.

Bennett, David H. *Bill Clinton: Building a Bridge to the New Millennium*. Routledge, 2014.

Bennet, William J. *Children's Book of Virtues*. Simon and Schuster, 1995

Bernstein, R.B. *Thomas Jefferson*. Oxford Press, 2003.

Beveridge, Albert J. *Abe Lincoln in Indiana*. Public Library of Fort Wayne, 1958.

Black, Conrad. *Richard M. Nixon: A Life in Full*. Public Affairs, 2008.

Blair, Gwenda.*The Trumps*. Simon and Schuster, 2001.

Booraem, Hendrik. *Young Gerry Ford: Athlete and Citizen*. Eerdmans Publishing, 2013.

Booraem, Hendrik. *Child of the Revolution: William Henry Harrison*. Kent State University Press, 2013.

Borneman, Walter R. *Polk: The Man Who Transformed the Presidency*. Random House, 2009.

Brinkley, Douglas. *Gerald R. Ford*. Henry Holt and Company, 2007.

Brands, H.W. *Andrew Jackson: His Life and Times*. Random House, 2006.

Brands, H.W. *Reagan: The Life*. Doubleday, 2015.

Brenner, Martha. *Abe Lincoln's Hat*. Random House, 1994.

Brinkley, Alan. *John F. Kennedy*. Henry Holt and Company, 2012.

Brisbin, James Sanks. *From the Tow-Path to the White House: The Early Life and Public Career of James A. Garfield*. Hubbard Bros., 1880.

Broadwater, Jeff. *James Madison: A Son of Virginia and a Founder of the Nation*. University of N. Carolina Press, 2012.

Brodsky, Alyn. *Grover Cleveland: A Study in Character*. St. Martins Press, 2000.

Brookhiser, Richard. *James Madison*. Basic Books, 2011.

Brown, Hilton. From Introduction to *Benjamin Harrison: Hoosier Warrior*. American Political Biography Press, 1997.

Brown, William Garrott. *Andrew Jackson*. Houghton Mifflin Company, 1900.

Brunelli, Carol. *Zachary Taylor (Presidents of the U.S.A)*. Child's World, 2014.

Buller, Jon et al. *Smart About the Presidents*. Grosset & Dunlap, 2004.

Bunting, Josiah. *Ulysses S. Grant: The American Presidents Series*. Macmillan, 2004.

Burr, S.J. *The Life and Tomes of William Henry Harrison*. Ransom, 1840.

Busch, Julia. *John F. Kennedy, Retro Comics 14*. Anti-Aging Press, 2013.

Bush, Barbara. *A Memoir.* Scribner, 1994.

Bush, Doro. *My Father, My President: A Personal Account of the Life of George H. W. Bush.* Hachette Book Group, 2006.

Butterworth, Hezekiah. *True to his Home: A Tale of the Boyhood of Franklin Pierce.* D. Appleton Company, 1897.

Calhoun, Charles. *Benjamin Harrison: The American Presidents Series.* Macmillan, 2013.

Cannon, James. *Gerald R. Ford: An Honorable Life.* University of Michigan Press, 2013.

Caro, Richard A. *The Path to Power: The Years of Johnson I.* Vintage, 2011.

Carter, Jimmy. *An Hour Before Daylight: Memories of a Rural Boyhood.* Simon & Schuster, 2001

Cavanaugh, Frances. *Abe Lincoln Gets His Chance.* Rand McNannly and Company, 1959.

Chancellor, William Estabrook. *A Brief Biography if James Madison.* AJ Cornell Publications, 2012.

Chancellor, William Estabrook. *A Brief Biography of James Monroe.* A. J. Cornell Publications, 1912.

Chancellor, William Estabrook. *A Brief Biography of William McKinley.* Neale Publishing Co., 1912.

Chancellor, William Estabrook. *Warren Gamaliel Harding: President of the United States.* Sentinel Press, 1922.

Cheatham, Mark R. *Andrew Jackson, Southerner.* LSU Press, 2013.

Cheney, Lynne. *James Madison: A Life Reconsidered.* Viking, 2014.

Chernow, Ron. *Washington: A Life.* Penguin Books, 2010.

Chisholm, Hugh. *Andrew Johnson, 17th President—A Short Biography.* Shamrock Eden Publishing, 2011.

Chitwood, Oliver P. *John Tyler: Champion of the Old South.* American Historical Association, 1939.

Clements, Kendrick A. *Woodrow Wilson: World Statesman.* Endeavor Press, 2015.

Colbert, Nancy. *Great Society: The Story of Lyndon Baines Johnson.* Morgan Reynolds Publishing, 2002.

Collins, Gail. *William Henry Harrison.* Holt, 2012.

Coolidge, Calvin. *Autobiography of Calvin Coolidge.* Little & Ives, 1929.

Cooper, John Milton. *Woodrow Wilson.* Vintage, 2009.

Corey, Shana. *Barack Obama: Out of Many, One.* Random House, 2013.

Cramer, Richard Ben. *Being Poppy: A Portrait of George Herbert Walker Bush.* Simon & Schuster, 2013.

Cramer, Richard Ben. *What it Takes: The Road to the White House.* Random House, 1992.

Crapol, Edward. *John Tyler, the Accidental President*. University of North Carolina Press, 2006.

Crapol, Edward. *John Tyler, the Accidental President*. University of North Carolina Press, 2006.

Crockett, David. *The Life of Martin Van Buren*. Navish & Cornish, 1845.

Cuneo, Sherman. *From Printer to President*. Dorrance, 1922.

Cushing, Caleb. *Outlines of the Life and Public Services, Civil and Military, of William Henry Harrison*. Eldridge, 1840

D'Antonio, Michael. *The Truth About Trump*. Thomas Dunne Books, 2016.

Dallek, Robert. *An Unfinished Life: John F. Kennedy, 1917 – 1963*. Little, Brown and Company, 2003

Dallek, Robert. *Harry S. Truman: The American Presidents Series*. Macmillan, 2008.

Dallek, Robert. *Lyndon B. Johnson: Portrait of a President*. Oxford University Press, 2004.

Davis, Oscar King. *William Howard Taft: The Man of the Hour*. P.W. Zigler Co., 1908.

Dean, John W. *Warren G. Harding: American Presidents Series*. Times Books, 2004.

Deem, James. *Zachary Taylor*. Enslow, 2002.

Donaldson, Madeline. *Richard Nixon: History Maker*. Lerner Publishing, 2008.

Doherty, Kieran. *William Howard Taft: Encyclopedia of Presidents*. Children's Press, 2004.

Donovan, Sandra. *James Buchanan (Presidential Leaders)*. Lerner, 2005.

Drew, Elizabeth. *Richard M. Nixon: The American Presidents Series*. Macmillan, 2010.

Editors, Charles River Editions. *American Legends: The Life of Richard Nixon*. Charles River Editions, 2014.

Editors, Charles River Editions. *History for Kids: The Illustrated Life of Barack Obama*. Charles River Editors, 2013.

Editors, Charles River Editions. *History for Kids: The Illustrated Life of Thomas Jefferson*. Charles River Editions, 2013.

Editors of TIME. *Barack Obama: A Day in the Life of America's Leader*. TIME for Kids, 2009.

Edwards, Roberta. *Who is Barack Obama?* Grosset & Dunlap, 2009.

Eisenhower, John S.D. *Zachary Taylor: The American Presidents Series*. Henry Holt, 2008.

Ellis, Edward S. *Thomas Jefferson: A Character Sketch*. H.G. Campbell, 1898.

Ellis, Joseph J. *His Excellency: George Washington*. Vintage, 2004.

Elston, Heidi M.D. *Harry S. Truman*. ABDO Publishing Company, 2009.

Emmons, William. *Biography of Martin Van Buren—President of the United States*. Leeaf.com Classics, 2013.

Endicott, Michael. *Richard Nixon: A Man Nobody Knew*. Amazon Digital Services, 2013.

Evensen Lazo, Caroline. *Martin Van Buren*. Lerner, 2005.

Ferling, John. *John Adams: A Life*. Oxford University Press, 2010.

Ferling, John. *The Ascent of George Washington: The Hidden Political Genius of an American Icon*. Bloomsbury Press, 2009

Ferrell, Robert H. *Harry S. Truman: A Life (Give 'em Hell, Harry)*. University of Missouri Press, 1994.

Finkelman, Paul. *Millard Fillmore*. Macmillan, 2011.

Fiske, John. *President Tyler—A Short Biography*. Shamrock Eden Publishing, 2011.

Fleming, Thomas. *Truman*. New World City, 2014.

Foley, Michael. *Harry S. Truman*. Chelsea House, 2004.

Foster, Lillian. *Andrew Johnson: His Life and Speeches*. Richardson & Co., 1866.

Frisbee, Lucy Post. *John Fitzgerald Kennedy: America's Youngest President*. Aladdin Paperbacks, 1986.

Frith, Margaret. *Who was Franklin Roosevelt?* Grosset & Dunlap, 2010.

Frith, Margaret. *Who was Woodrow Wilson?* Grosset & Dunlap, 2015.

Fritz, Jean. *Bully for You, Teddy Roosevelt!* Putnam, 1991.

Fritz, Jean. *The Great Little Madison*. G. O. Putnam, 1989.

Frost, John. *The Life of Zachary Taylor*. D. Appleton & Co., 1847.

Fry, J. Reese. *A Life of Gen. Zachary Taylor; Comprising a Narrative of Events Connected with his Professional Career, Derived from Public Documents and Private Correspondence*. Grigg, Elliot & Co., 1848.

Gaines, Ann Graham. *Theodore Roosevelt*. The Child's World, 2002.

Gaines, Ann Graham. *Harry S. Truman: Our Thirty-third President*. Child's World, 2014.

Gartner, John. *In Search of Bill Clinton: A Psychological Biography*. Macmillan, 2008.

Gherman, Beverly. *Jimmy Carter (Presidential Leaders)*. Lerner, 2004.

Gordon-Reed, Annette. *Andrew Johnson: the American Presidents Series*.

Macmillan, 2011.

Gormley, Beatrice. *Barack Obama: Our 44th President*. Aladdin, 2012.

Gormley, Beatrice. *President George W. Bush: Our Forty-Third President*. Aladdin, 2000.

Gould, Lewis. *The William Howard Taft Presidency*. University Press of Kansas, 2009.

Gottfried, Ted. *Millard Fillmore: Presidents and Their Times*. Cavendish Square Publishing, 2007.

Graff, Henry F. *Grover Cleveland (The America Presidents Series)*. Henry Holt, 2002.

Gutzman, Kevin R.C. *James Madison and the Making of America*. St. Martins, 2012.

Halbert, Patricia. *I Wish I Knew That: U.S. Presidents*. Readers Digest, 2012.

Hamilton, Nigel. *Bill Clinton: An American Journey*. Random House, 2003.

Hamilton, Nigel. *JFK: Reckless Youth*. Random House, 1992.

Hamilton, Nigel. *The Mantle of Command: FDR at War, 1941-1942*. Houghton Mifflin, 2014.

Harness, Cheryl. *Young John Quincy*. Bradbury Press, 1994.

Harper, Brett. *Kennedy*. New Word City, 2015.

Harper, Brett. *Roosevelt*. New Word City, 2014.

Harris, John. *The Survivor: Bill Clinton in the White House*. Random House, 2005.

Hart, Gary. *James Monroe: The American Presidents Series*. Times Books, 2005.

Havelin, Kate. *Andrew Johnson*. Lerner, 2005.

Hawthorne, Nathaniel. *The Life of Franklin Pierce*. Ticknor, Reed and Fields, 1852.

Hitchens, Christopher. *Thomas Jefferson (Eminent Lives)*. HarperCollins, 2009.

Holt, Michael. *Franklin Piece: The American Presidents Series*. Macmillan, 2010.

Hopkinson, Deborah. *John Adams Speaks for Freedom*. Simon Spotlight, 2005.

Hoogenboom, Ari. *Rutherford B. Hayes: Warrior and President*. University Press of Kansas, 1995.

Icke Anderson, Judith. *William Howard Taft: An Intimate Portrait*. WW Norton, 1981.

Irving, Washington. *George Washington: A Biography*. G. P. Putman & Sons, 1876.

Isecke, Harriet. *Lyndon B. Johnson: A Texan in the White House*. Teacher

Created Materials, 2012.

Jackson, Isaac R. *The Life of William Henry Harrison, the People's Candidate for the Presidency.* C. Sherman & Co. Printers, 1840.

Jeansonne, Glen. *The Life of Herbert Hoover.* Palgrave Macmillan, 2012.

Jones, James S. *Life of Andrew Johnson: Seventeenth President of the United States.* East Tennessee Publishing Co., 1901.

Kalman, Maira. *Thomas Jefferson: Life, Liberty, and the Pursuit of Everything.* Penguin, 2014.

Kaplan, Fred. *John Quincy Adams: American Visionary.* HarperCollins, 2014.

Karabell, Zachary. *Chester Alan Arthur.* Henry Holt, 2004.

Kearns Goodwyn, Doris. *The Bully Pulpit: Theodore Roosevelt, William Howard Taft, and the Golden Age of Journalism.* Simon & Schuster, 2013.

Kearns Goodwyn, Doris. *Lyndon Johnson and the American Dream.* Harper & Row, 1976.

Kellogg, Veron. *Herbert Hoover: The Man and His Work.* Heritage Books, 2009.

Kent, Zachary. *Theodore Roosevelt: Twenty-Six President of the United States.* Children's Press, 1988.

Kent, Zachary. *Encyclopedia of Presidents: Ronald Reagan.* Children's Press, 1989.

Ketchum, Richard M. *George Washington.* New World City, 2015.

Klingel, Cynthia and Noyed, Robert B. *Ronald Reagan: Our Fortieth President.* The Child's World, 2002.

Korda, Michael. *Ulysses S. Grant: The Unlikely Hero.* HarperCollins, 2013.

Kengor, Paul. *God and George W. Bush: A Spiritual Life.* Harper, 2004.

Kent, Zachary. *Ulysses Grant: Encyclopedia of President.* Children's Press, 1989.

Kerly, Barbara and Fothergham, Edwin. *Those Rebels, John and Tom.* Scholastic Press, 2012.

Ketcham, Ralph. *James Madison: A Biography.* Macmillan, 1971.

Knight, C.J. *Abraham Lincoln: An Overview of the Exciting Achievements of a Great U.S. President and Example of Leadership.* Amazon Digital Service, 2015.

Kranish, Michael and Marc Fisher. *Trump Revealed.* Scribner, 2016.

Krensky, Stephen. *DK Biography: Barack Obama.* DK Children, 2009.

Krull, Kathleen. *A Boy Named FDR: How Franklin D. Roosevelt Grew Up to Change America.* Knopf, 2013.

Landau, Elaine. *Warren G. Harding.* Lerner Publications Company, 2005.

Lassieur, Allison. *James Buchanan*. Children's Press, 2004.

Levy, Debbie. *Rutherford B. Hayes (Presidential Leaders)*. Lerner, 2006.

Leonard, Thomas M. *James K. Polk: A Clear and Unquestionable Destiny*. SR Books, 2001.

Liggett, Walter W. *The Rise of Herbert Hoover*. The H.K. Fly Company, 1932.

Logan Hollihan, Kerrie. *Theodore Roosevelt for Kids: His Life and Times*. Chicago Review Press, 2010.

Lurie, Jonathan. *William Howard Taft: The Travails of a Progressive Conservative*. Cambridge University Press, 2011.

Maraniss, David. *First in His Class: A biography of Bill Clinton*. Simon & Schuster, 2008.

Marquez, Heron. *George W. Bush (Presidential Leaders)*. Twenty First Century Books, 2006.

May, Gary. *John Tyler: The American Presidents Series*. Macmillan, 2008.

McCullough, David. *John Adams*. Simon & Schuster, 2001.

McCullough, David. *Truman*. Simon and Schuster, 2003.

McCollum, Sean. *John Quincy Adams: Encyclopedia of Presidents*. Children's Press, 2003.

McCormac, Eugene Irving. *James K. Polk: A Political Biography*. University of California Press, 1922.

McElhiney, Thomas. *Life of Martin Van Buren*. J. T. Shryock, 1853.

Meacham, Jon. *American Lion: Andrew Jackson in the White House*. Random House, 2009.

Meacham, Jon. *Destiny and Power: The American Odyssey of George Herbert Walker Bush*. Random House, 2015.

Melady, Thomas Patrick. "George Bush: Influence of the Family on His Values" from *A Noble Calling: Character and the George H.W. Bush Presidency*. Praeger, 2004.

Mendel, David. *Obama: A Promise of Change*. HarperCollins, 2008.

Merwin, Henry Childs. *Thomas Jefferson*. Houghton Mifflin, 1901.

Miller, Brandon Marie. *Thomas Jefferson for Kids: His Life and Times*. Chicago Review Press, 2011.

www.millercenter.org

Miller, Nathan. *Theodore Roosevelt: A Life*. Morrow, 1992.

Minutaglio, Bill. *First Son: Georg W. Bush and the Bush Family Dynasty*. Random House, 2001.

Mitchell, Barbara. *Father of the Constitution: A Story about James Madison*. First Avenue Editions, 2004.

Montgomery, Henry. *The Life of Major General Zachary Taylor, Twelfth President of the United States*. Derby, Miller & Co., 1849.

Morgan, George. *The Life of James Monroe*. Small, Maynard and

Company, 1921.

Morgan, H. Wayne. *William McKinley and His America*. Kent State University Press, 2002.

Moriarty, V.G. *Eisenhower: The President*. Amazon Digital Services, 2014.

Morris, Edmund. *Theodre Rex*. Random House, 2001.

Morris, Edmund. *The Rise of Theodore Roosevelt*. Coward, McCann & Geoghegan, 1979.

Morse, John Torrey. *John Adams*. Houghton Mifflin, 1889.

Naftali, Timothy. *George H.W. Bush*. Henry Holt and Company, 2007.

Nelson, Michael and Perry, Barbara (eds.). *41: Inside the Presidency of George H.W. Bush*. Cornell University Press, 2014.

Nikel, Jim. *The First Gay President? A look into the Life and Sexuality of James Buchanan, Jr.* Minute Help Press, 2011.

O'Brien, Michael. *John F. Kennedy*. St. Martin's Press, 2005.

Ochester, Betsy. *George Bush: Encyclopedia of Presidents*. Children's Press, 2005.

Ogg, Frederic Austin. *The Reign of Andrew Jackson*. Yale University Press, 1919.

Olcott, Charles S. *The Life of William McKinley*. Houghton Mifflin, 1916.

O'Riley, Bill and Martin Dugard. *Killing Reagan: The Violent Assault That Changed a Presidency*. Henry Holt and Company, 2015.

Pafford, John. *The Forgotten Conservative: Rediscovering Grover Cleveland*. Regnery History, 2013.

Pascal, Janet. *Who Was Abraham Lincoln?* Grosset & Dunlap, 2008.

Patterson, Raymond. *Taft's Training for the Presidency*. Chapple Press, 1908.

Peckham, Howard. *William Henry Harrison: Young Tippecanoe*. Patria Press, 2003.

Peskin, Allan. *Garfield*. Kent State University Press, 1978.

Peters, Charles. *Lyndon B. Johnson: The American Presidents Series*. Simon and Schuster, 2010.

Pietrusza, David. *Calvin Coolidge: A Documentary Biography*. Church & Reid Books, 2013.

Potts, Steve. *Kennedy: A Photo-Illustrated Biography*. Bridgestone Books, 1996.

Rappaport, Doreen. *To Dare Mighty Things*. Hyperion Books, 2013.

Raum, Elizabeth. *Gift of Peace: The Jimmy Carter Story*. Zonderkidz, 2011.

Rayback, Robert J. *Millard Fillmore: Biography of a President*. American Political Biography Press, 1992.

Reagan, Ronald. *An American Life.* Simon and Schuster, 1990.

Riehecky, Janet. *Ulysses S. Grant: Encyclopedia of Presidents.* Children's Press, 2004.

Remnick, David. *The Bridge: The Life and Rise of Barack Obama.* Knopf, 2010.

Roberts, Jeremy. *James Madison (Presidential Leaders).* Lerner Publishing Group, 2003.

Rosenbush, James. Tr*ue Reagan: What Made Ronald Reagan Great and Why it Matters.* Center Street (Hachette Book Group), 2016.

Rountree, Clarke. *George W. Bush: A Biography.* Greenwood Books, 2010.

Rove, Karl. *The Triumph of William McKinley.* Simon & Schuster, 2015.

Ruth, Amy. *Herbert Hoover.* Lerner Publications, 2004.

Sandburg, Carl. *Abe Lincoln Grows Up.* Harcourt Brace & Co., 1956 (reprint from *The Prairie Years,* 1928).

Scarry, Robert J. *Millard Fillmore.* McFarland & Company, 2001.

Schaller, Michael. *Ronald Reagan.* Oxford University Press, 2010.

Schurz, Carl. *Rutherford B. Hayes—A Short Biography.* Shamrock Eden Publishing, 2011.

Schultz, B.J. *The Life of Thomas Jefferson.* Amazon Digital Services, 2013.

Schwartzman, Paul and Michael E. Miller. "Confident. Incorrigible. Bully: Little Donny was a Lot Like Candidate Donald Trump" *Washington Post,* June 22, 2016.

Shapiro, Marc. *Trump This!* Riverdale Avenue Books, 2016.

Shlaes, Amity. *Coolidge.* HarperCollins, 2013.

Shepard, Edward M. *Martin Van Buren.* Houghton, Mifflin & Co., 1899.

Sievers, Harry J. *Benjamin Harrison: Hoosier Warrior.* American Political Biography Press, 1952.

Smith, Jean Edward. *Bush.* Simon & Schuster, 2016.

Smith, Jean Edward. *Eisenhower in War and Peace.* Random House, 2012.

Sobel, Robert. *Coolidge: An American Enigma.* Regnery History, 2012.

Stein, R. Conrad. *Calvin Coolidge: Encyclopedia of Presidents.* Children's Press, 2004.

Stanley, George E. and Henderson, Meryl. *Harry S. Truman: Thirty-third President of the United States.* Aladdin, 2010.

Stanley, George E. *Andrew Jackson: Young Patriot.* Aladdin Paperbacks, 2003.

Sterne Randall, William. *Thomas Jefferson: A Life.* New World City, 2014.

Stewart, Marsha. *Warren G. Harding (Death by Blackness)*. Conquering Books, 2005.

Stoddard, William O. *Grover Cleveland*. 1888.

Sutcliffe, Jane. *Barack Obama (History Maker Bios)*. Lerner Publications, 2010.

Sutcliffe, Jane. *John Adams*. Lerner, 2006.

Takiff, Michael. *A Complicated Man: The Life of Bill Clinton as Told by Those Who Know Him*. Yale University Press, 2010.

Tarpley, Webster and Chaitkin, Anton. *George Bush: The unauthorized Biography*. Progressive Press, 2004.

Thomas, Evan. *Being Nixon: A Man Divided*. Random House, 2015.

Thomas, Garen. *Yes We Can: A Biography of President Barack Obama*. Macmillan, 2010.

Tierney, Tom. *Ronald Reagan: Paper Dolls in Full Color*. Dover Originals, 1984.

Tobin, James. *The Man He Became: How FDR Defied Polio to Win the Presidency*. Simon & Schuster, reprint 2013.

Todd, Chuck. *The Stranger: Barack Obama in the White House*. Little Brown, 2014.

Trefousse Hans L. *Andrew Johnson: A Biography*. W.W. Norton, 1989.

Trefousse, Hans. *Rutherford B. Hayes*. Henry Holt, 2002.

Trinh, David. *Bill Clinton: A Biography*. Hyperink Originals, 2012.

Trump, Donald with Tony Schwartz. *Trump: The Art of the Deal*. Random House, 1987.

Various authors. *James Madison: An Abridged Biography*. Amazon Digital Services, 2013.

Unger, Harlow Giles. *The Last Founding Father: James Monroe and a Nation's Call to Greatness*. Da Capo Press, 2009.

Venezia, Mike. *Andrew Jackson: Seventh President*. Children's Press, 2005.

Venezia, Mike. *Benjamin Harrison: Getting to Know the U.S. Presidents*. Children's Press, 2006.

Venezia, Mike. *George Bush: Forty-First President 1989-1993*. Children's Press, 2008.

Venezia, Mike. *Gerald R. Ford: Thirty-Eighth President 1974-1977*. Children's Press, 2008.

Venezia, Mike. *Getting to Know the U.S. Presidents: Bill Clinton*. Children's Press, 2007.

Venezia, Mike. *Getting to Know the U.S. Presidents: George W. Bush*. Children's Press, 2008.

Venezia, Mike. *Getting to Know the U.S. Presidents: Jimmy Carter*. Children's Press, 2008.

Venezia, Mike. *Getting to Know the U.S. Presidents: John Quincy Adams*.

Children's Press, 2004.

Venezia, Mike. *Getting to Know the U.S. Presidents: Ronald Reagan.* Children's Press, 2008.

Venezia, Mike *James K. Polk: Eleventh President.* Scholastic, 2005.

Venezia, Mike. *James Monroe: Fifth President.* Children's Press, 2005.

Venezia, Mike. *Martin Van Buren: Eighth President.* Children's Press, 2005.

Venezia, Mike. *William Henry Harrison: Ninth President.* Children's Press, 2005

Venezia, Mike. *William Howard Taft: Twenty-Seventh President.* Children's Press, 2007.

Walker, Jane C. *John Tyler: A President of Many Firsts.* McDonald & Woodward, 2001.

Washington, Austin. *The Education of George Washington.* Regnery History, 2014

Waxman, Laura Hamilton. *Gerald Ford.* Lerner, 2008.

Waxman, Laura Hamilton. *Jimmy Carter.* Lerner, 2006.

Weiner, Tim. *One Man Against the World: The Tragedy of Richard Nixon.* Henry Holt, 2015.

Weiss, Ellen and Friedman, Mel. *Jimmy Carter: Champion of Peach.* Aladdin, 2003.

Welch, Catherine A. *George H.W. Bush.* Lerner Publications, 2008.

White, Ronald C. *A. Lincoln: A Biography.* Random House, 2009.

White, William Allen. *A Puritan in Babylon: The Story of Calvin Coolidge.* Macmillan, 1938.

Whitelaw, Nancy. *Jimmy Carter: President and Peacemaker.* Morgan Reynolds, 2004.

Whitelaw, Nancy. *Theodore Roosevelt Takes Charge.* Albert Whitman & Company, 1992.

Wicker, Tom. *Dwight D. Eisenhower.* Henry Holt and Company, 2002.

Widmer, Ted. *Martin Van Buren.* Henry Holt and Company, 2005.

www.wikipedia.org

Williams, Jean Kinney. *Benjamin Harrison: Encyclopedia of Presidents.* Children's Press, 2004.

Wills, Gary. *James Madison.* Henry Holt and Company, LLC, 2002.

Woods, Randall. *LBJ: Architect of American Ambition.* Free Press, 2006.

Winglet, Mary Mueller. *Gerald R. Ford.* 21st Century Books, 2007.

Winters, Kay. *Abe Lincoln: The Boy Who Loved Books.* Aladdin, 2006.

Yager, Edward M. *Ronald Reagan's Journey: Democrat to Republican.* Rowman & Littlefield, 2006.

Zelizer, Julian E. *Jimmy Carter.* Henry Holt, 2010.

Zimmerman, W.F. *A Brief Biography of Franklin Pierce, 14th President of the United States.* A.J. Cornell Publications 2014

Zimmerman, W. F. *A Brief Biography of Martin Van Buren, Eighth President of the United States.* A.J. Cornell, 2013.

About the author

William Walsh is the author of four books of fiction and nonfiction. His texts and stories have been widely published.

CPSIA information can be obtained
at www.ICGtesting.com
Printed in the USA
BVOW05s1207090117
472989BV00006B/6/P